I paid all my debts....

A Norwegian-American Immigrant Saga of Life on the Prairie of North Dakota

Lloyd A. Svendsbye

D1453412

Lutheran University Press
Minneapolis, Minnesota

I paid all my debts. . . .

A Norwegian-American Immigrant Saga
of Life on the Prairie of North Dakota

by Lloyd A. Svendsbye

Copyright 2009 Lloyd Svendsbye. All rights reserved

Library of Congress Cataloging-in-Publication Data

Svendsbye, Lloyd (Lloyd August), 1930-
I paid all my debts : a Norwegian-American immigrant saga of life on the
prairie of North Dakota / Lloyd A. Svendsbye.
   p. cm.
Includes bibliographical references and index.
ISBN-13: 978-1-932688-41-2 (alk. paper)
ISBN-10: 1-932688-41-2 (alk. paper)
   1. Svendsbye, Anders A. (Anders Andersen), 1882-1967—Family. 2.
Svendsbye, Gudrun, 1901-1968. 3. Birkelo, Thor, 1863-1941. 4. Birkelo,
Gjertru, 1861-1939. 5. Svendsbye, Lloyd (Lloyd August), 1930—Family.
6. Norwegian Americans—North Dakota—Biography. 7. Immigrants—
North Dakota—Biography. 8. Pioneers—North Dakota—Biography. 9.
Frontier and pioneer life—North Dakota. 10. Tioga (N.D.)—Biography. I.
Title.
   F645.S2S85 2009
   978.4'0309233982—dc22
                                          2009026366

Fourth Printing 4 5 6 7 8 9 10

Lutheran University Press, PO Box 390759, Minneapolis, MN 55439
www.lutheranupress.org
Manufactured in the United States of America

Dedication

To my parents,
Anders and Gudrun Svendsbye,
whose integrity shone like a beacon

Table of Contents

Preface

This is a book about two immigrant families from Norway whose dreams of economic betterment turned into near disaster. Their saga needs to be told because the experience of immigrants is often romanticized into success stories. Not all families enjoyed that romance. For some, tragedy struck in the middle of the first dance.

The narrative begins in Norway in the communities of Krøderen and Byrkjelo. Krøderen, from which Anders came, is nearly sixty miles west and a bit north of Oslo; Byrkjelo, the homeland of Thor, Gertru, and Gudrun, is on Norway's west coast, about halfway between Bergen to the south and Trondheim to the north. The story continues in Williams County in northwestern North Dakota, to which both families immigrated in 1904. They were part of the last wave of the population explosion that hit the United States in the nineteenth and early twentieth centuries, fed largely by European migration. The two families were a part of the more than 800,000 Norwegian immigrants who joined over thirty-four million other immigrants who flooded the shores of the U.S.A. from 1815 to 1915.

The work uses a variety of means to tell a story that actually happened. It does not allow imagination to exploit nor intrude on the accuracy of the account as it unfolds on the North Dakota prairie. The family narratives are largely chronological, though not rigidly so. They are not a memoir, although personal memory plays a significant part in a few of the last chapters. However, the memoirs are corrected and informed by historical research, which makes each of the episodes historically accurate and verifiable.

The families are those of Anders and Gudrun Svendsbye, who are my parents, and Thor and Gjertru Birkelo, who are my maternal grandparents, with particular attention to the life and experience of Anders and Gudrun. Since they are my family, I become a minor player in some of the episodes toward the end of the book. Hopefully that contributes to the saga and gives readers a realistic insight into the personal pathos and struggle each of the immigrants experienced.

The family story is filled with high hopes and deep despair. The hopes arose in Norway as each family was tantalized by the lure of the prairie—160 acres of free land. The despair developed out of failed economic expectations in the United States, fueled most dramatically by drought and Depression, but also by farm consolidations and changes in transportation. The downward side began in 1919, continued into the 1920s when crops were poor half of the time, and continued through the 1930s when the crops were consistently poor. The drought brought on a rural depression that predated the nation's and world's Great Depression by a decade, with dire consequences for the immigrants.

Like thousands of other Norwegians, the Svendsbye and Birkelo families left mountains, valleys, and fjords to cross the Atlantic in search of a better economic life. They came to a flat prairie that they expected to have soil rich enough to bring them relative prosperity. They struggled heroically in tilling the soil. But the twin disasters of nature (drought) and the economy (Depression) wiped out one family and nearly derailed the other.

The Svendsbye-Birkelo story was shared by thousands of immigrants who left their homelands with the same economic quest in mind. It reflects both the strength of the immigrants' dreams and determination and the harsh realities that dogged them as they tirelessly cultivated the soil, trying to translate hopes into realities. Such is the heritage from which many Americans came.

My chief purpose in writing this book is to help contemporary Americans to better understand what it was like to live in rural Norway and immigrate to the Upper Midwest of the United States about a century ago. What did pioneer life on the prairie look like and feel like? My hope is that the book, by illuminating the past, may help some people identify, claim, and celebrate their own roots, and that many others will simply enjoy the story.

Williams County today has a serious problem of declining population. But despite that fact, many people who live there like it and have no intention of leaving—ever. Similarly, Anders and Gudrun Svendsbye never thought seriously about leaving. The Birkelos ended up so impoverished, they could not have left had they wanted to. This is a story about extraordinary perseverance and devotion to the land—their own and the prairie around them—despite all odds.

Lloyd Svendsbye
Summer 2009

SWEDEN

VERDAL •
• LEVANGER

• TRONDHEIM
•SKOGN

NORDFJORDEID •

• BYRKJELO

NORWAY

• BERGEN
KRØDEREN • • OSLO

• STAVANGER

• KRISTIANSAND

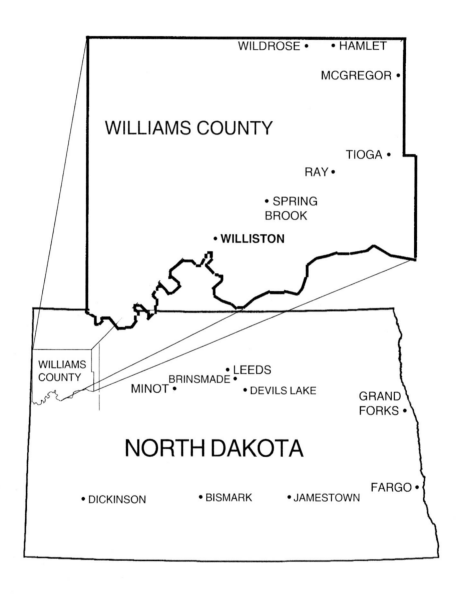

Chronology

This chronology is provided to enable the reader to follow the events in the narrative.

1824   December 10—Stephen Kristofferson Bjørkelo, my maternal great-grandfather, was born in the Breim Parish of Gloppen Township of Sogn og Fjordane County.

1829   Katrine Daviddatter Sandal, my maternal great-grandmother, was born in the same township and county.

1851   Anders Svendsby, my paternal grandfather, was born near Krøderen.

1853   Steffen Bjørkelo and Katrine Sandal, my maternal great-grandparents, are married. They had five children, all of whom immigrated to the U.S.A.

1854   December 25—Kristi Bjørkelo was born in Breim. Married Ragnald Flugekvam, immigrating to the U.S.A. and homesteading near Edinburg, North Dakota.

1856   Marit Stensrud Juvet, my paternal grandmother, was born.

1858   Anne Bjørkelo was born October 31 in Breim. She immigrated with her brother, Thor, to Williams County, North Dakota.

1861   April 6—Gjertru Serine Johannesdatter Øvrelid was born at Nordfjordeid.

1861   April 14—Kristen Bjørkelo was born in Breim. He immigrated to North Dakota and moved to the state of Washington where he worked as a carpenter.

1863   April 16—Thor Bjørkelo was born on the Bjørkelo farm just outside of Byrkjelo in Gloppen Township of Sogn og Fjordane County.

1866   February 8—Steffen Bjørkelo was born.

Events from the Birkelo (Bjørkelo) family are recorded here in regular type.

Events from the Svendsbye (Svendsbye) family are recorded in italic type.

Events shaping the world and the Birkelo/Svendsbye family lives are recorded in sans serif type.

1876 *November 12—Lina Hovemoen, Anders Svendsbye's first wife, was born.*

1880 *January 30—Anders Svendsbye and Marit Stensrud, my paternal grandparents, were married in the Olberg Kirke in Krøderen. They took the name Stryken from the farm on which they lived. They had seven children whose functioning surnames* changed as the family moved from farm to farm.*

1880 *August 24—Gina Andersdatter Stryken* was born.*

1882 *March 18—Anders Andersen Stryken*, my father, was born.*

1884 *October 6—Elling Andersen Medrud* was born.*

1887 *January 29—Gustav Andersen Medrud* was born.*

1887 March 7— Thor Bjørkelo married Gjertru Øvrelid in the church in Byrkjelo.

1887 April 18— Synnove Torsdatter Bjørkelo was born. In the U.S.A., she first took the name Sena and then May.

1887 October 6—The Great Northern Railroad reached Williston, North Dakota.

1889 February 6— Kamille Torsdatter Bjørkelo was born. In the U.S.A., she took the name Calma.

1889 *March 26—Marie Andersdatter Tangane* was born.*

1891 *June 6—Martha Andersdatter Tangane* was born.*

1891 August 3—Jenny Mathilde Torsdatter Bjørkelo was born. In the U.S.A., she spelled her name Jennie.

1893 August 30— Margit Torsdatter Bjørkelo was born. In the U.S.A. she took the name Margaret and married Horatio Dean Nelson. They had five children.

1895 September 27— Sigurd Bjørkelo was born.

1896 *June 24—Ole Andersen Tangane* was born.*

1896 *Anders and Marit Stryken purchased the Svendsby farm near Snarum and gave the name Svendsby to all their children.*

1897 March 12—Inga Bjørkelo was born.

1900 February 22—Theodore Bjørkelo was born.

1900 F. D. Hankey started ranching 3-½ miles south of what came to be Hamlet, North Dakota.

1901   September 19—Gudrun Johanna Bjørkelo was born in Lavanger, north of Trondheim, Nord-Trøndelag County.

1902   The Hankey School was opened on the J.D. Hankey ranch.

1902   The village of Tioga was established on the main line of the Great Northern Railroad.

1903   *July—Lina Hovemoen immigrated first to Devils Lake and then to Williams County in northwestern North Dakota.*

1904   Thor Bjørkelo, with his two oldest children, Synnove and Kamille, and his sister, Anne, immigrated to Williams County, North Dakota, where they homesteaded near Hamlet.

1904   June 7—Thor and his sister, Anne, went to Minot to file their intent to become U.S. citizens and to file for homesteads on the southeast quarter and the southwest quarter of section 11 of what was to become Big Meadow Township.

1905   Gjertru Bjørkelo, wife of Thor, immigrated with their other six children: Jenny (Jennie), Margit (Margret), Sigurd, Inga, Theodore, Gudrun.

1905   June 20—Grong Lutheran Church was formed.

1906   June 3—Trinity Lutheran Church was organized about 2-½ miles north of where Hamlet would be located.

1907   December 12—Thor and Anne's homestead filings cleared.

1908,   Easter Sunday—Thor's sod house was gutted by fire. In the summer of that year, Thor and Gjertru negotiated their first loan in the U.S.A. to buy their homestead and build a house.

1908,   July—Anne Birkelo died a pauper.

1908   *Anders bought a new Deering binder for $60.00 and remained in debt almost until his death.*

1910   January—Big Meadow Township was organized.

1910   A post office named Hankey was opened on the J.D. Hankey ranch.

1910   Hamlet post office opened.

1911-1916—Great Northern Railroad built a spur from Stanley to Grenora.

1911   Great Northern Railroad spur reached McGregor, Hamlet and Wildrose.

1911   June—McGregor village was organized.

1911   November—Businesses from Paddington moved adjacent to railroad, and the Great Northern renamed the village Wildrose.

1911-1914—Hamlet School was opened.

1912   June 22—Anders Svendsbye and Lina Hovemoen were married.

1914   May 10—Margaret Svendsbye was born to Anders and Lina.

1915   Lina Hovemoen Svendsbye died.

1918   December 5—Anders Svendsbye and Gudrun Birkelo were married in Wildrose, North Dakota.

1919   December—Thor and Gjertru Birkelo negotiated two loans totaling $4,506; $2,500 was borrowed from the McGregor State Bank which sold the mortgage to Kinyon Investment Company of Owatonna, Minnesota.

Early 1920s—Depression began in farm communities of North Dakota.

1923   Thanksgiving Day—The new Hamlet School was dedicated. The following year, it opened as a twelve-grade school.

1925   March 4—Kinyon foreclosed on Birkelos' mortgage. The Birkelos were forced off their homestead to live in a two-room shack for the remainder of their lives. Williams County Sheriff sold the farm at auction.

1929   World Depression began.

1930   Ten year drought followed. Farmers evacuated the prairie.

1932   Franklin Delano Roosevelt elected president.

1940   Anders began to repay his debt.

1941   Rains returned solidly; crops were excellent. Anders had 135-foot well drilled.

1942   Hamlet School reduced to eight grades.

1948   Rural Electrification Administration brought electricity to farms.

1949   Mechanization of Svendsbye farm began with purchase of a tractor.

1957   Trinity Lutheran Church disbanded.

1960   Hamlet School closed.

1962   Anders completed payment of his debts.

1964   Anders and Gudrun moved to Tioga. For the first time in sixty years, they had running water.

1967   May 30—Anders died in Tioga Hospital.

1967   Grong Lutheran Church closed.

1968   March 18—Gudrun died in Tioga Hospital.

Genealogy

This genealogy is provided to enable the reader to keep track of the relationships of the persons in the narrative.

Maternal Side

Stephen Kristofferson Bjørkelo—Katrine Daviddatter Sandal
    Kristi (Christine) Steffendatter Bjørkelo—Ragnald Flugekvam
    Anne Steffendatter Bjørkelo
    Kristen Steffenson Bjørkelo
    Thor Steffenson Bjørkelo—Gjertru Serine Øvrelid
        Synnove (who took the name Sena)
        Kamille (who took the name Calma)
        Jenny Mathilde
            Harry Juston, out of wedlock. Adopted (Gail Allen Phillips).
            Jennnie later married Martin Christopherson.
    Margit (Margaret) Bjørkelo—Horatio Dean Nelson
    Sigurd Bjørkelo
    Inga Bjørkelo
    Theodore Bjørkelo
    Gudrun Johanna Bjørkelo—Anders A. Svendsbye
    Steffen Steffenson Bjørkelo

Paternal Side

Anders Andersen—Gjertrud Olsdatter
    Anders Andersen—Marit Ellingsdatter

They had seven children whose functioning surnames changed as the family moved from farm to farm. In 1898, Anders and Marit bought the Svendsby farm near Snarum and gave all their children the name Svendsby.

Gina Andersdatter Stryken
Anders Andersen Stryken—(1) Lina Hovemoen
    Margaret—Gilmer Vatne

Anders Andersen Stryken Svendsbye—(2) Gudrun Johanna Birkelo
    Alice Gertrude Svendsbye—Art Vatne
    Albert Theodore Svendsbye
    Lillian Irene Svendsbye—Rodney Nelson
    Gladys Sophie Svendsbye—Arthur Berg
    Ida Geneva Svendsbye—Eugene Benson
    Lloyd August Svendsbye—Annelotte F. E. Moertelmeyer
    Adeline Lenora Svendsbye—Harry Elverud
    Edward Gilbert Svendsbye
    Jean Kay Svendsbye—Marlowe Brusven

CHAPTER 1

From Norway to North Dakota

All over Norway in the last half of the nineteenth century, ordinary people were talking about free land in America available to anyone who could put together enough money to get there. At that time, the USA had more land available for settlement than any other country in the world. By the time George Washington became president, the boundaries claimed by the new nation extended as far west as the Mississippi River. The boundary lines were moved further west when President Jefferson, in 1803, arranged to buy 891,363 square miles of land from France for $15 million, which was less than three cents per acre. Known as the Louisiana Purchase, it was the largest acquisition of territory without war in the western world. It included the large sections of prairie between the Mississippi and the Rocky Mountains. To encourage settlement of that area, President Abraham Lincoln signed into law an act of Congress known as the Homestead Act on May 20, 1862. It offered 160 acres of free land to any citizen who was at least twenty-one years of age or had served in the US army or navy, or a foreign born person of the same age, simply by paying a $10.00 filing fee and agreeing to build a house, dig a well and live on the land for five years while cultivating a few acres of land.

The rural folk in Norway were particularly interested in that land because there was not enough room in Norway for generation after generation to plan a life of farming. Among those lured by the promise of land was Anders A. Svendsbye, a young man working in the forest and on his parents' farm west of Oslo, and Thor and Gjertru Birkelo, a married couple living in Levanger, north of Trondheim, where Thor was among the laborers then building Norway's railway system.

Anders Svendsbye (1882-1967)

Anders Svendsby, as he wrote his name after his parents bought the Svendsby farm in 1896, grew up in the area of Krøderen, about sixty miles west and a bit north of Oslo.[1] The farms of the region were small and were nestled among large acreages of forest. For at least two hundred years, Anders Svendsby's forebears had lived in this area as manual laborers, working on farms as tenants or cotters. As cotters they had done manual work for a farm owner in exchange for the use of land and the right to dwell on it. In the second half of the nineteenth century, some of them worked in the timber industry and on the railroad.

Beginning in the middle of the eighteenth century, these forebears worked on the lower Glesne farm just south of Krøderen. At that time, the Glesne farm was relatively large and subdivided into units bearing such names as Stryken, Medrud, and Tangane. Stryken [rapids] was considered a good place to live, having a comparatively large number of animals.[2] In 1865 Stryken had one horse, four cows, and nine sheep. By comparison, Tangane had three cows and three sheep.

My paternal grandparents, Anders Andersen Stryken and Marit Ellingsdatter Stensrud, whose photographs suggest sober-faced folk, were living on the Stryken farm when they were married at Olberg Kirke in Krøderen on January 30, 1880. While Anders worked on the railroad and together with Marit looked after crops

Anders Andersen Stryken and Marit Stensrud Stryken, parents of Anders A. Svendsbye

and animals, children began to arrive. Eventually there were seven of them: four boys and three girls. Anders, my father, was the oldest of the boys and was born on the Stryken farm just south of Krøderen on March 18, 1882. The next two boys, Elling and Gustav, were born on the Medrud farm, a neighboring farm to which the family had moved some months after Anders' birth. Ole, the youngest son and youngest child, was born on the Tangane farm, also a neighboring farm, to which the family moved after the birth of daughter Marie. The girls were all born on different farms. Gina, the oldest child, was born on Stryken, Marie on Medrud, and Martha on Tangane.

One of the consequences of moving from farm to farm was that family names functioning as surnames could change with the move to each farm. Prior to 1923 when the national parliament passed the Naming Act, surnames were not required in Norway. Before that time, children in rural

Stryken farm home in Krødsherad Township, Buskerud County, Norway, where Anders Svendsbye was born.

areas were generally identified as the sons or daughters of their father or mother or as someone living on a certain farm. Thus my father Anders wound up having four different names functioning as surnames while he lived in Norway. He was baptized Anders Andersen, that is, Anders, son of Anders. At fifteen months when he was vaccinated for smallpox after his parents had moved to the Medrud farm, his name was recorded as "Anders Andersen Medrud born in Krødshered of the parents Anders Andersen Medrud and his wife Marit Ellingsdatter and living in Krødshered." Later, when his family moved to Tangane, he took the name Anders Andersen Tangane. He was given the Svendsby surname in 1898 when his parents bought the Svendsby farm, just six years before he emigrated.

The children of the growing family attended the public school. Anders was enrolled in the Fyrand School, a two-room school in the northern part of Krødshered Township from 1889 to 1896. When he started school, there were ten weeks of school each year, but the school term had expanded to fourteen weeks by the time he graduated. The academic year started October 1 and ended May 1, with the first five to seven weeks in October and November, and the last five to seven in March and April. That schedule allowed the children to be at home during the coldest and snowiest part of the winter as well as during the growing season.

The curriculum was specific and substantial. Each week there were nine hours of reading, nine of religion, two of singing, five of writing,

Fyrand School in Krødsherad Township, Buskerud County, Norway, where Anders Svendsbye attended school.

five of arithmetic, and three hours each in new subjects such as history, geography, and biology, for a total of thirty-nine hours; in addition, some time was devoted to drawing. Eight hours of classes a day for five days a week would make forty hours, without allowance for additional study time. Anders did well in school, according to the records. When he graduated in 1896, he was given these grades, with one being the highest on a scale of one to six: reading, 1.5; religion, 1.5; writing, 1.8; arithmetic, 1; singing, 1.5; geography, 1.5; history, 1.5; biology, 1.5 and drawing, 2.

The nine hours a week studying religion fulfilled a national requirement that major attention be given to the study of Martin Luther's Small Catechism. That requirement was in conformity with the 1814 Norwegian Constitution, which stated that "The Evangelical Lutheran religion shall remain the public religion of the State. The inhabitants professing it shall be required to bring their children up in the same." Both the constitution and the laws implementing it were modified beginning in 1851. Completion of the study of the Catechism in public school prepared Anders for confirmation in 1896 in the Olberg Kirke of Krøderen, where his parents had been married and he had been baptized. After completing elementary education and being confirmed, he likely worked for two years in the Krøderen community until his parents bought a farm and moved the family there.

Anders and Marit Stryken became landowners in their own right in 1898 when they purchased the Svendsby farm, about a dozen miles south from where they were living. That act reflected a get-ahead attitude that their children inherited, whether they crossed the Atlantic or remained in Norway. The farm had been in existence at least since the beginning of the sixteenth century. The name means "Sven's town." The spelling of the name changed through the years until 1886 when the current spelling used in Norway—Svendsby—was adopted.[3]

The Svendsby farm lay in a mostly wooded area. The tree-covered mountains were low and inviting to hunters and skiers as well as farmers. With the Snarum River running only a few feet from the farmhouse, the countryside was fertile and inviting. The large house, which had been erected in 1750, was constructed of one-foot-square logs formed by hand from trees in the nearby forest where men, using axes, cut down the trees, shaped them into logs, and transported them to the farm on horse-drawn conveyances.[4]

Like many other families, the Svendsby family earned its livelihood through a combination of occupations. The father and two sons, for example, were away from home when the census of 1900 was taken. When the census taker arrived, Anders and his two oldest sons were at work in the forests felling trees and making the timber ready to be floated down the Snarum River to Drammen or hauled by horses to a sawmill. Women maintained the farms in the absence of their men, and Marit Stensrud Stryken, Anders' wife, is listed in the census as being in charge of the house and the cattle barn. The oldest daughter, Gina, is listed as employed by her parents on the farm.

Oral tradition has it that Anders had a girlfriend from Krøderen whom the Svendsby family liked very much. Apparently she came from one of Krøderen's "better" families. Her parents did not want her to emigrate, however, and nothing came of the romance. The lure of the prairie, and the economic future of the United States, seems to have captured Anders' imagination more than the prospect of marriage in Norway. However inadequate their income may have been at the time, Anders and his brother Elling Andersen Svendsby earned and saved enough money so that by 1904 and 1905, respectively, they could travel to the United States. Anders was likely employed at least part-time for nine years before leaving for America.

Anders did not leave a record of the factors influencing his decision to emigrate. He certainly knew of the abundant land available in the United States. He knew the promise of a better living than he might obtain in Norway. He knew friends in America. He may also have wished to avoid military service. He was certainly an avid reader of newspapers, and they

Olberg Kirke in Krødsherad Township, Buskerud County, Norway, where Anders Stryken and Marit Stensrud were married and Anders Svendsbye was baptized and confirmed.

were regularly full of news about the United States. Anders was twenty-two years old when he emigrated in 1904, but his earnings had been so meager that he must have worked for several years to earn and save enough money for ocean and train transportation from Snarum, Norway, to Leeds, North Dakota. His ocean travel cost $53.30, and his rail travel in the United States cost $47.70. He had $60.00 in cash when he arrived in the United States. Anders must have had to save the equivalent of perhaps $250.00 to pay those and miscellaneous other costs. This data suggests his decision to emigrate was made during his teens.

Anders had probably never been to Oslo, known then as Christiania. Hence he was likely seeing Norway's capital city for his first and only time. The railroad took him directly to the dock where the Montebello was moored. After shepherding his trunk to the departure area, he boarded the ship and was soon sailing south in the Oslofjord. He likely joined hundreds of other Norwegians lining the rails to see their homeland for the last time. The first stop was at Hull, on England's east coast. There he

The Celtic on which Anders Svendsbye arrived in New York from Norway on July 30, 1904.

disembarked to take a train across that country, through some of its most important industrial centers, to Liverpool. In the Liverpool harbor Anders first glimpsed the majestic Celtic, the largest ocean liner then in existence. The Celtic left Liverpool on July 16, 1904, with Anders A. Svendsbye, as he later decided to spell his name, aboard.

As the Celtic approached the southern tip of Manhattan and the White Star Line's Hudson River piers, it passed first the Statue of Liberty, then Ellis Island, where the immigrants traveling in third class would be taken soon after landing.[5] The Statue of Liberty, a gift of France to the United States, had been erected in 1885. Anders perhaps had read or heard about the nation's words of welcome—"Give me your tired, your poor, your huddled masses yearning to be free"—from Emma Lazarus' poem "The New Colossus," which had been affixed to the statue's pedestal in 1901, three years before Anders' arrival in the United States.[6] He almost certainly had no idea that the ore for the statue's copper had been mined in Norway.[7]

Thor Birkelo (1863-1941) and Gjertru Serine Johannesdatter Øvrelid (1861-1939)

The Bjørkelo—or Birkelo—family had lived for more than four centuries on the Bjørkelo farm just outside of Byrkjelo. The farm was located in the Breim Parish of Gloppen Township in the Sogn og Fjordane County on Norway's western coast, midway between Bergen and Trondheim. The Bjørkelo farm is situated in a valley surrounded by mountains, their tops

The valley in the Sogn og Fjordane County of Norway in which Thor Birkelo was born and grew up.

capped most of the year by snow, which, when melting, feeds the many streams that tumble down the mountainside into the nearby lakes and fjords.

The parents of the Bjørkelos who emigrated to Dakota were Steffen Kristofferson Bjørkelo and Katrine Davidsdatter Sandal. Steffen was a farmer

The house in Nordfjordeid in the Eid parish of the More og Romsdal County in Norway where Gjertru Øvrelid Birkelo, mother of Gudrun Svendsbye, was born.

and also a tailor. Both Steffen and Katrine were born in the 1820s and were raised in the same community. They had five children; two girls and three boys, all of whom emigrated to the United States. The second of their three sons, Thor, was born on April 16, 1863, and baptized two days later in the Breim parish. He learned independence early. He was nine when his father died and fifteen when his mother died. Even though elementary education was made mandatory in Norway three years before he was born, he did not attend school. He remained in the Byrkjelo community after the deaths of his parents; he worked on farms and helped build and maintain roads in the area.

On March 7, 1887, Thor was married in the white, wooden church in the Breim parish, where he had been baptized. He married Gjertru Serine Johannesdatter Øvrelid, from Nordfjordeid. Gjertru had been born on April 6, 1861, in Nordfjordeid, a short distance northwest of Byrkjelo. The Øvrelid home in which Gjertru was born was nestled against mountains on one side and overlooked the deep Nordfjord on the other. Gjertru's father, Johannes Jonson Øvrelid, was a carpenter who farmed a small acreage. He and his wife, Marte Hendricksdatter Haugland, had a family of ten children, four of whom immigrated to the United States.

As close as Byrkjelo and Nordfjordeid were to each other, they were separated by a mountain range that had to be crossed on foot. This fact spurs one to ask how Thor and Gjertru became acquainted. Perhaps one or both worked for a time in the other's community. However and wher-

The Nordfjord, a few feet below the house in which Gjertru Birkelo was born.

ever Thor and Gjertru met, she was eight months pregnant when she and Thor were married. Despite Breim parish records listing their marriage as March 7, 1887, there was confusion later among the Birkelo children in the United States about the date of Thor and Gjertru's wedding. Two daughters, Inga and May (daughter Synnove had changed her name, first to Sena, then to May), corresponded about when to celebrate their parents' golden wedding anniversary. On November 18, 1935, May wrote Inga: "You asked about when Mother and Father were married. Well I am pretty sure it was on March 7, 1886. Because I know they were married more than one year when I was born. And I was born on April 18, 1887, so that makes their Golden Wedding next year."[8] The confusion is compounded by obituaries for both husband and wife. These reports indicate that they were married in 1885.[9] In any case, in Norway during the latter part of the nineteenth century, pregnancy prior to marriage was not uncommon, as the pioneer sociologist Eilert Sundt noted and as church records with the frequent notation *uaegte*, or illegitimate, make plain. Anders Svendsbye's mother, Marit Stensrud Stryken, had in fact also been pregnant when she and Anders Andersen Stryken were married in 1880.

The so-called "America Fever" had already struck the Birkelo family by the time Thor and Gjertru were married. The first of the Bjørkelos to emigrate was Thor's oldest sister, Kristi, who with her husband Ragnald Flugekvam had settled on a homestead in Sylvesta Township of Walsh County, North Dakota. The Flugekvam home near Edinburg became a stopping-off place for other members of the Bjørkelo family who came later. The second member of the Bjørkelo family to arrive in the United States was Kristen Steffen Bjørkelo, who left Bergen on July 28, 1885, arriving in Philadelphia in August. He went immediately to Edinburg, North Dakota, to the home of his sister Kristi Flugekvam, and remained there for at least a year doing manual labor. Later he settled in Vancouver, Washington, where he worked successfully as a carpenter.

Nearly twenty years passed before additional members of the Bjørkelo family emigrated. By that time, Thor and Gjertru had tried hard to make a go of it in Norway. They had lived for eight years in or near Byrkjelo before they began their restless journey northward in search of better economic circumstances. They spent a few years in and around Sunnyleven, a community of thirty-six residents situated at the east end of Storbjordenfjord near Geiranger. At the time of the baptism of their fifth child in 1895, they were living on the Tryggestad farm, just outside Sunnyleven, while Thor was a road worker, or *veiarbeider*. By 1897 they were living as the second family on the Bredheim farm in the Romsdal area. Sometime later they learned of new employment opportunities building the railroad north from Trondheim. At the time of the 1900 Norwegian census, the family of nine was living as a second family in the home of Ole and Oline Krøgstad in Skogn, about thirty miles north of Trondheim. Within a year the Bjørkelos were living five miles farther north at Levanger, where their youngest daughter, Gudrun, was born on September 19, 1901.

Even though Thor was employed full time, he earned barely enough money to support his family. Railroad workers at the time were paid only 3.2 kroner per day—unless they handled the dynamite for blasting rock. At that rate, Thor would have earned less than 1,000 kroner annually. Translated into U.S. currency at the time, Thor, working six days a week, living away from home in a windowless barracks provided by the railroad, earned about $1 per day.

The future in Norway seemed bleak. Thor had worked hard all his life to support himself, beginning when he was orphaned at age fifteen. What did he have to offer a potential employer? Never having gone to a school of any kind, he was uneducated and untrained in any profession. His only tools were a pick and shovel. He had used those tools in back-breaking labor for twenty-five years to build and maintain community roads and railroads, but many people could use a pick and shovel, and there was no shortage of laborers. The prospects seemed dim for increasing wages in an economy where there were more than enough workers for the available jobs. To break the bonds of poverty required radical action. They took it.

Under those circumstances, Thor and Gjertru decided to emigrate. They were considerably older than most emigrants of this period. Thor was forty-one and Gjertru forty-four. They had been married seventeen years and had eight children, ages three to seventeen. Given the parents' ages and with so large a family, their reasons for emigrating must have been compelling. They likely compared their circumstances with the stories in letters about Kristi's relative wellbeing on a homestead near Edinburg, North Dakota, and Kristen's financial success as a carpenter in the state of Washington.

But how could they manage the journey? Despite the hopeful prospects in America, Thor and Gjertru did not have the necessary money. Among other things, they decided that the family would not all emigrate together. This represented a major commitment to a better future. Thor would go first, with their two oldest daughters, Synnove and Kamilla. They would locate and prepare a place on the prairie. Gjertru and the other six children would remain in Norway for an additional year. For that last year, they moved a half-dozen miles farther north to Verdal. Thor's brother Kristen came to the rescue with funds. In 1909, he filed a sworn statement in the state of Washington stating that on February 23, 1904, he paid $205.50 for tickets for Thor, Synnove, and Kamilla to travel from Norway to Edinburg, North Dakota, and that a year later he provided $280.00 in cash to pay for tickets for "Mrs. Thor Birkelo and seven children" to come from Norway to North Dakota. That $485.50 loaned to Thor was to be interest-free for five years. The statement about seven children was in error; only six siblings were then living in Norway. In the 1910 U.S. census, Thor and Gjertru are recorded as having had nine children. Inga, born in 1897, had a twin sister, Ingrid, who died at birth.

The money from Kristen covered the bulk of immigration travel costs. The cost to Thor, Synnove, and Kamilla for their ship passage from Trondheim to New York was 120 kroner each. Rail travel for three from New York to St. Paul, Minnesota, would probably have cost something over $100. Backed by the generosity of brother and uncle, Thor and his two oldest daughters boarded the Salmo, a ship of the Stjernelinie, when it left Trondheim on April 6, 1904. The ship stopped at Bergen, where Thor's youngest sister, Anne, identified in the ship's documents as a domestic, joined them. They arrived in New York about a week later.

To Tioga

On the morning of July 30, 1904, the sun was shining brightly in a nearly cloudless sky as the Celtic was secured to its White Star Line pier in lower Manhattan. At 8:04 a.m. the temperature was an inviting sixty-eight degrees Fahrenheit. A light east wind gusting up to ten miles an hour drifted gently across the harbor, welcoming the immigrants to the new land.[10] Anders Svendsby's journey from Liverpool across the Atlantic to New York had lasted a little more than a week.

The immigrant was a handsome young man. He was lean and some-what muscular, with perfect posture and a good head of hair. When he later became a U.S. citizen, he was described in court papers as five feet, ten inches tall, white, with fair complexion, blue eyes, and light colored hair. He and other immigrants debarked the Celtic and boarded a ferry that took them to Ellis Island, where they entered the main building through the ground-floor baggage room. There they left their trunks and other baggage until they had completed the admissions process. From the ground floor, they

Anders A. Svendsbye in about 1910.

proceeded up a wide flight of stairs to the Great Hall. At the top of the stairs each was given a quick medical examination. Then they all waited to be interviewed by legal inspectors. Anders had to prove he could legally enter the United States. He had to have proof of his country of origin and show the U.S. government where he was intending to go and what work he planned to do.

While on Ellis Island, Anders made his first important decision in the United States. He changed his name. It was not an unusual exercise for Anders and other Norwegians; they were accustomed to altering their names in Norway, but this time he made a decision to settle on a name to use in America. On the manifest of the Celtic, he was registered as Anders Andersen Svendsby. Now, in Ellis Island's Great Hall, he dropped his middle name for the initial A, added an e to his surname, and signed his name as Anders A. Svendsbye.[11] He went by this name for the rest of his days.

Once admitted to the United States, Anders exchanged his Norwegian kroner for sixty U.S. dollars. Then he picked up his luggage and boarded another ferry for the mainland. His destination was Williams County, North Dakota, in the extreme northwestern corner of the state. His immediate destination, however, was Leeds, North Dakota, about 150 miles east of Williams County, where he would meet a friend. No record of that journey has survived except the date of his arrival in Leeds. His most seamless route, avoiding a change of stations in Chicago, would have had him take a ferry from Ellis Island to Jersey City, New Jersey, at the time the eastern terminus of the Pennsylvania Railroad.[12] There he would have boarded a train that would have taken him to Chicago's Union Station. But if he traveled on the New York Central from New York to Chicago, he likely would have taken a ferry from Ellis Island back to Manhattan and its Grand Central Station. On the New York Central he would have arrived at Chicago's LaSalle Street Station, which would have required getting himself and his trunk to Union Station. Whatever his route to Chicago, once there he likely boarded a Burlington or Milwaukee train to St. Paul. There, at 7:55 p.m., he boarded a Great Northern train to Leeds.

It probably took Anders Svendsbye four days to travel from New York to Leeds. Transferring from the Celtic to ferries and then from train to train cannot have been easy for the newcomer, not least because Anders had a wooden trunk, sixteen inches wide, two feet long, and twenty-one inches deep containing everything he owned, except for the clothes he wore and the money he carried. With only sixty dollars in his pocket when he left Ellis Island, he had to watch his money carefully. He likely traveled as cheaply as possible and caught sleep when and where he could, and he probably bought meager food along the way in New York or at stops en-route.

Anders arrived in Leeds at 2:04 p.m. on August 30, a beautiful summer day. The mid-afternoon sky was clear and the sun was shining, and the temperature was in the lower seventies. It may have rained later that evening. Given the amount of rainfall in the region that summer, North Dakota must have looked its greenest and best as it welcomed its new resident.

Anders was met by his friend Olaus Svendsbye, not a relative but a countryman from the same part of Norway. Olaus had settled near Brinsmade, about twelve miles east and south of Leeds. Anders worked there for several weeks, likely hired to help with the harvest. Since the rainfall received in the area that year was six inches above normal, the wheat and other grain fields must have been thick and beautiful. He remained with Olaus until November, when he boarded a Great Northern train in Leeds for his trip to Tioga, in Williams County, which cost him $5.46.

In Tioga, Anders was met by another friend, Knute Berg. Born in Norway the same year as Anders, Knute left Norway in 1896 at age fourteen, coming to Detroit, Michigan. From Detroit he went to Brinsmade, North Dakota, where he lived for a few years before filing for his homestead northwest of Tioga the year before Anders arrived. In all likelihood, he invited Anders to stay at his house, because the land Anders selected was only one mile west of Knute's homestead. Anders chose land in Township 159 North, Range 96 West. His choice made, he boarded the train from Tioga to Minot on the night of November 16 to complete arrangements. The train trip to Minot cost $2.46.

Arriving in Minot, Anders stayed overnight. The following day, November 17, he likely rose early to go to the state's Eighth District Court.[13] There, before C. H. Thorpe, deputy clerk of court, he swore that it was his bona fide intention "to become a citizen of the United States, and to renounce forever all allegiance and fidelity to any Foreign Prince, Potentate, State or Sovereignty, whatever, and particularly to the government of the King of Norway and Sweden": it was necessary to renounce allegiance to both nations.[14] That duty completed, he went to the U.S. Department of the Interior Land Office in Minot to file his homestead claim. He selected the NE ¼ of the SE ¼ of Section 15 and the W ½ of the SW ¼ and the SW ¼ of the NW ¼ of Section 14, Township 159 North, Range 96 West.

Not only did he sign his intent to become a US citizen, which he was required to do before he could file for a homestead, he also was required to sign several other documents. Among them was a Non-Mineral Affidavit in which Anders swore that "no portion" of his homestead was "claimed for mining purposes" and that his application was "not made for the purpose of fraudulently obtaining title to mineral land but with the object of securing land for agricultural purposes."[15] Following that, he signed a Homestead Affidavit that said he was applying for free land only for himself and "not for the benefit of any other person, persons or corporation."[16] That done, he paid a $14.00 fee to pay for the entry of his homestead numbered 30589 in the United States Record. The trek from Norway to the United States, which Anders had made in order to claim 160 acres of free land, had ended, and his new life had begun. He then left for the Midwest forests to work during the winter.

To Big Meadow Township

Thor Birkelo and his daughters Synnove and Kamilla, together with his sister Anne, arrived in New York in mid-April 1904. From there they traveled to Edinburg, North Dakota, to stay with Thor's sister Kristi Flugekvam, whom Thor and Anne had not seen since Kristi had emigrated eighteen years earlier. By June, Thor and Anne had selected land in Township 159 North, Range 96 West, which later became Big Meadow Township. They returned to Minot on June 7 to register their intent to file for citizenship and make their homestead claims.

They likely arrived permanently at their homestead site (in the future Big Meadow Township) in early June after filing papers in Minot and immediately began constructing a sod house on Thor's land. The barn could wait until another year, because they probably had no animals yet. Thor's house was probably built in the southeast corner of the homestead. A small slough in that part of the land would have provided good sod for building and would have been relatively free of rock.

By October 1, Anne, who also claimed a quarter-section homestead, had spent $60 to construct what the record calls "two shacks," one with a shingled roof and another with only plain lumber for the roof. They were constructed back-to-back to form a ten-by-twenty-foot house. Later she arranged the construction of a fourteen-foot square sod barn with a straw roof and the digging of a well that was twenty-two feet deep. She valued her property at $250.

The Birkelos probably lived in a tent while they built their first house. The nearest neighbors at any rate, Knute Berg and Frank Hankey, lived more than a mile away. Food and other supplies had to be brought from Tioga, some twenty miles away. They were probably compelled at first to hire the McGregor Livery Service to provide a pair of horses and a wagon to transport themselves and their goods to their land. Later, neighbors would shop for one another whenever they made the long trek to town.

Having arrived on the prairie, where did they get water to drink, cook, and bathe before they dug their wells? Historians say that pioneers obtained their water from rivers and sloughs. How far did the Birkelos have to walk to find such a slough? If they were removing sod from the small slough close to where their house was being built, that slough likely did not provide potable water. A fairly deeper slough lay a mile south of the Birkelos. They might have walked there, or they might have walked the one mile to the home of Knute Berg and carried pails of water back to their home from either the slough or from Knute's well. When it came to washing clothes, even somewhat distant neighbors may have collaborated. Francis Fryckman, writing in the Williams County history, says that,

> When washday came around, three neighbor homesteaders (all women) would carry their wash tubs, boilers, washboards and laundry to the nearest slough with water. There they built a fire with twigs and cow chips near the edge of the slough, heated the water, and did their washing–spreading the clothes on the grass or bushes to dry.[17]

They also needed fuel for fires. There were no forests. There was lignite coal, but it was more than twenty miles away, and they likely had no transportation of their own until the following year. Carrying goods on one's back while walking was not uncommon at that time in Norway or the Midwest. Is that how Thor provided for his family in 1904?

Having lived that first summer in a tent on the prairie and constructing their sod house, there were other preparations to be made for winter before the hard frost. Arriving in late May or early June, they undoubtedly planted potatoes and some other vegetables to be harvested in the fall. Potatoes, carrots, onions, and other root crops could be stored for months. Acquiring the potatoes and the vegetable seeds to be planted required another long trip to Tioga—by foot if horses were not available. With no land yet broken, they had to use a spade to turn over the prairie by hand for their garden. Their work had surely begun.

CHAPTER 2

Newcomers

To the new immigrants, the contrasts in geography must have been striking. Their native land had jagged mountains covered with trees; streams gushed down into valleys and into a river that flowed past only a few feet from their home. They came to Tioga to follow a dream. Now it lay before them. Their homesteads in the extreme northwestern part of North Dakota were generally flat, with few hills or trees in sight, grass waving mile after mile across the prairie. If strange at first, this would be the home of Thor and Gjertru Birkelo and Anders Svendsbye for the rest of their lives.

Emerging Communities

With the July 1887 arrival of the Great Northern Railway in Williston, the county seat of Williams County, settlers—chiefly ranchers—began moving into the area surrounding the future site of Tioga. The village was established in 1902, although it was not incorporated until 1910. Nickolas W. Comford bought the land from men who had received it as compensation for service in the U.S. Army. Comford was employed by the Great Northern railroad to locate town sites. Having selected the site for Tioga, he purchased the land to sell it to prospective residents and profit from his location decision. He sold it to Nels W. Simon, who in turn sold lots to immigrants.[1]

The first structure in Tioga was a boxcar that was used as a train station, occupied by two section foremen and their families. Shortly after the arrival of that boxcar, the railroad erected a small building where section workers lived, most of them Japanese. Lumber for the first two businesses to open in Tioga in 1902 came from White Earth, thirteen miles east of Tioga. The first was a lumberyard owned by W. H. Dixon. Dixon, who operated his lumberyard with his brother Joe, was born in Indiana and had run cattle on the prairie near Wilmot, South Dakota, as well as working for a few years as an agent for the railroads in various North

The Nels Simon Store built in Tioga, North Dakota, in 1902.

Dakota towns. Later, he opened another lumberyard in nearby McGregor. The lumberyard was quickly followed by a general store built by Nels W. Simon. Nels Simon, who provided the principal leadership to found and build Tioga, was born in Sweden in 1865 and as a small boy emigrated to the United States with his parents. They settled in Illinois, then moved to Iowa, and later to Benson, Minnesota. From Benson, Nels shipped all his belongings in two rented boxcars to Tioga early in 1902. He rented the boxcars from the Great Northern Railway, which made them available at a low price to immigrants to transport their goods. Riding in the cars with the animals, furniture, and equipment were Nels' two oldest sons. "Immigrant cars," as they were popularly called, were an inexpensive way to transport family, personal belongings, furniture, horses, cattle, wagons, harnesses, and small machines like walking plows. The *Tioga Gazette* reported that 108 immigrant cars were shipped to Tioga in 1904 and 167 cars during the first nine months of 1905.

Simon's store provided groceries, clothing, and hardware. It also served as the first post office, with Simon as the first postmaster, beginning December 6, 1902. Part of the building's second floor, accessible by means of an outside stairway, was used for one year as the first school. The school then moved to another temporary space until a separate structure was built in 1904. The second-story space of the Simon building was also used as a community room for lodge meetings, dances, lectures, traveling shows, political meetings, and Roman Catholic worship.

In 1903, several new businesses were established in Tioga. Rev. M. D. Whitmore built a hotel so that homesteaders would have a place to stay when they arrived. Whitmore was the first schoolteacher in Tioga; he homesteaded southeast of town. The McGregor brothers built the first livery barn and later sold it to John and Ole Neset, who also helped homesteaders settle on their claims. John Amundson started a blacksmith shop. A printing shop was opened and began publishing the *Tioga Gazette*. A barbershop, a pharmacy, a pool hall, a hardware store, and one or more restaurants followed. Soon there came a tailor shop, a harness shop, and a meat market. The first bank opened in 1904 as the Tioga State Bank, with William McClintock as cashier. That same year the first grain elevator was built in Tioga. In its first year, it shipped out 10,840 bushels of flax and 2,350 bushels of wheat. An important new arrival on the scene in 1906 was Dr. Robert Stobie. He visited the sick in their homes in town or on their farms, driving a horse and buggy in the summer and a one-horse sleigh in winter. He was soon followed by a dentist and a veterinarian. Businesses and institutions, including the predictable jail, multiplied in later years. Of great importance was the establishment in 1908 of the Simon Brothers' Implement Company, making International Harvester machinery available to the community.

The Tioga School, built in 1908.

New to American ways, Thor and Gjertru Birkelo managed to find their way. The record is silent about this. The U.S. Land Office in Williston advertised in the *Tioga Gazette* that personnel came to Tioga two times each month to assist homesteaders with a variety of issues. Among the service offered was help in identifying available land. According to a document filed on December 5, 1905, in the Land Office in Williston, Thor Birkelo hired Lewis Larson of White Earth to drive him to what later was named Big Meadow Township to select his homestead land. Anne, Sena, and Calma may also have accompanied him, because Anne also chose a quarter section on which to homestead, adjacent to Thor. They selected land about fifteen miles northwest of Tioga.

The area was not yet organized when Thor and Gjertru Birkelo and Anders Svendsbye arrived, although the land had been surveyed and platted. The three towns that were to be most important in their lives— Hamlet, McGregor, and Wildrose—were not yet in existence. Tioga had been established only two years earlier.

The process of organizing the township, in fact, created a stir in the community. A petition was addressed to "the Hon. Board of County Commissioners of Williams County" on November 15, 1909, signed by C. J. Sween and twenty-four others, constituting "a majority of the legal voters of Congressional Township 159, Range 96, . . . which township contains twenty-five or more legal voters." They petitioned the "honorable board to . . . forthwith proceed to fix and determine the boundary of such new township and to name the same Big Meadow."[2] On the original copy of the petition, the name Big Meadow was crossed out in green ink and the name Stordahl inserted. Stordahl—Norwegian for big valley—appears in the typed copy of the petition filed with the county commissioners.

Big Meadow Township

The reason for the change is not given in the minutes, but one can put the pieces together.

At a meeting of the commissioners on January 6, 1910, a motion to approve the petition and its boundary designations was unanimously passed. Also approved that day was a motion instructing the "citizens of

Stordahl Township" to meet in "the school house" (presumably Hankey) at 9:00 a.m. on February 7 to elect eleven officers. County Sheriff E. R. Olson hired a livery service to drive him to Big Meadow Township to post three notices to inform the citizens of the forthcoming election. He submitted a bill to the County Commissioners for $18.25 to pay for costs as follows: posting three notices, 75 cents; to travel 115 miles, $11.50; and livery hire for two days, $6.00.

By the time the county commissioners met on February 14, something had happened to change their minds. C. J. (Carl) Helle, who lived in the township and had moved the approval of the name Stordahl in January, now moved to change the name from Stordahl to Big Meadow.

Helle was much concerned with the name of the township. Stordahl (or its variants Stordal, Stordalen or Størdalshalsen) was the name of the community near Trondheim, Norway, from which he came. The name Stordahl was used for the first post office in the township, as well as for the Norwegian Lutheran Church, which was organized in Helle's home and built on land he gave the congregation. At the same time, twenty-five of his neighbors had originally petitioned the county commissioners to name the township Big Meadow. When those neighbors learned of the change to Stordahl, they descended on Helle and lobbied him to have the name changed back to what was originally requested. While there is no record of what transpired in the month between the two commission meetings, the record is clear that on February 14, Helle made the motion to change the original decision from Stordahl to Big Meadow. The will of the majority prevailed.[3]

The English language and American topography triumphed over the Norwegian tongue and remembered geography. Big Meadow Township got its name from the large meadow that covered three thousand of the twenty-three thousand acres in the township. The Williams County history writers suggest that the meadow was the largest of its kind in North Dakota. It was under water much of the time and grew wild hay that the farmers cut and harvested. It produced as much as three to four tons of hay per acre, so in a good year it could produce twelve thousand tons of hay, bringing buyers to the area from miles around.

Three supervisors and other township officers were elected at the February organizational meeting. Frank Hankey, Edward Iverson, and Hugh Smith were named supervisors. Bernhard Roll was elected treasurer; Carl Sween, clerk; Hjelmer Loe, assessor; Olaf Netmanger and Charles J. Helle, justices of the peace; Olaf Smith and Elias O. Strand, constables; and Christ Holl, overseer. Governance at the most local level had now come to the pioneer community, and the citizens had witnessed how democracy worked as they struggled with one another to name the township. A plurality of the officers (five out of eleven) had been born in Norway. Three others were of Norwegian descent. The remaining three were of Swiss, Swedish, and English descent. All three of the supervisors had been born in the U.S. All of the officers were farmers.

The Birkelos Struggle to Secure Ownership of the Land

Thor and Gjertru Birkelo were not the first to homestead in the future Big Meadow Township. Prior to 1900 there were at least four ranchers in the community: Frank Hankey, August Biwer, O. O. Adams, and Frank Thompson. In addition to C. J. Helle, a few others had arrived in 1902. Homesteading increased considerably after that year. Thor and his sister Anne had arrived in 1904. A year later, Gjertru Birkelo and her six other children arrived in the United States. They sailed from Trondheim on March 22 on the Salmo of the Wilson Line, to England, where they transferred to a ship of the Cunard Line, which brought them to Boston. From there, they went by rail and/or steamboat to Duluth, Minnesota—Superior, Wisconsin to visit Gjertru's sister, Marie Hoven, and her oldest brother, now named Lars Johnson. Thor came to Superior to welcome Gjertru and the children to the United States and accompany them to the future Big Meadow Township. In the late spring or early summer of 1905, Gjertru and her six children arrived in Tioga with Thor.

There they saw their fourteen-by-eighteen-foot sod house for the first time. There were now ten people to occupy that small space. Since Anne had completed construction of her frame house the previous fall, some of the girls could have stayed with her. How did the large family organize itself to sleep in this tiny house? Did they all ever sit down to eat at the same time? Did they share dishes or eat, in the old Norwegian fashion, out of common bowls? How did they wash and how did they keep clothes on their backs? We do not know, but it can only have been an enormous task to live one day at a time with so large a brood in such circumstances.

It is impossible to reconstruct the shape of life in this family, but some recollections of what the father and mother were like have survived. Thor was something of a recluse. He had not learned to read. They had no newspapers. He loved to drive his horses at top speed, especially when driving his buggy. Once when he was raking hay, his horses got away from him and ran out of control. He was thrown from the hay rake and broke a leg. It was never set by a physician and healed so badly that he had a crooked leg and thereafter walked with a limp. Gjertru was slightly taller than Thor and a bit stout. She planted a large garden to feed her family. She milked cows and sold cream and butter to earn a few dollars. She had a reputation as a marvelous cook and in later years regularly made lefse for church dinners. Lefse, a substitute for bread, was made of diced potatoes, flour, and cream, with salt and sugar added, along with but-

Thor and Gjertru Birkelo, fall of 1938.

ter, if it was available. It was made in the shape of a pancake and baked on top of the kitchen stove. In addition to taking care of her family, she was a midwife who delivered many babies. She was a *kloke kone* in the Norwegian tradition and precursor of the community nurse, who often went to area farm homes to help care for the sick. Sometimes in that process she would bake bread or wash clothes as needed by the families she served. Gjertru worked hard during the flu epidemic of 1918, walking from neighbor to neighbor to help care for the sick. In that epidemic, two neighbors—Ida Strand Olson and Edward Strand—died three days apart and were buried in a double funeral.

The financial records maintained by Thor's brother Kristen tell us something about the development of the Birkelo farm. On December 2, 1905, Kristen advanced Thor $275 to buy two horses, $99 to purchase a wagon and plow and $38.50 to buy harnesses for the horses. Thor came to his homestead in the summer of 1904. If it were necessary to pay cash for his horses, harnesses, and wagon, he would not have been able to buy them until the beginning of the winter of 1905. On the other hand, if he were able to buy them on credit, which is likely, he could have acquired them in 1904, then borrowed the money from his brother a year later to pay for those first important purchases. Not until the next year did Thor purchase a cow. Kristen loaned him $36.50 on March 23, 1906, to buy one. Again on April 25, 1907, Kristen loaned Thor $225.00 to buy a second team of horses.

Legal as well as financial problems soon beset the Birkelos. On June 7, 1904, Thor and Anne went to Minot to file for their homesteads. Thor thought he was filing for the SE ¼ of Section 11, and Anne thought she was filing for the SW¼. But the documents, still on file with the Interior Department's Land Office, clearly state that they applied for the opposite quarter sections from what they intended. Both applications were filled out by Minot Land Office staff, who mistakenly filled in the wrong names for the two quarter sections.

Almost a year and a half later, on December 5, 1905, Thor and Anne appeared in the Land Office in Williston to amend the original documents. Being duly sworn, they told their stories. Thor testified that he was person number 28337, who had filed for homestead on the SW ¼ of Section 11 on June 7, 1904. He testified that a mistake had been made by persons "at Minot in the office." He stated that while he had intended to file for the SE ¼ of Section 11 in Township 159 North, Range 96 West, "they" had mistakenly indicated he was filing "on the claim my sister would have," namely, the SW ¼. He swore that he had not noticed the error and had learned about it only when his brother-in-law, Ragnald A. Flugekvam, "by chance saw it on papers." Thor signed his application to amend with an X.[4] Anne signed a similar statement to amend her application number 28338 for the SW ¼ of Section 11, also swearing that the "office at Minot, N.D." mistakenly recorded that she was filing for the land her brother wanted.[5]

More than two months passed after Thor and Anne reported the mistakes to the Williston Land Office before the government took its first step. On its face, the problem should have appeared minor. The Land Office only needed to change a W to an E and an E to a W. But apparently nobody in Williston or Minot was authorized to make even so small a correction. Therefore, the matter was referred to Washington, D.C. Five months later, the Washington office wrote saying that if an error had been made, the Minot office should give Thor and Anne sixty days in which to fill out the application forms they had enclosed.

On September 7, 1906, the Williston Land Office committed a second mistake. They wrote letters to Anne and Thor that were intended to inform them that their applications to amend had been approved. But the letters were never delivered due to incorrect addresses. The letters were sent by registered mail to each of the applicants at "Williston, N.D." The Birkelos' correct address was Stordahl. When the addressees could not be found in Williston, the letters were returned to that city's U.S. Land Office.[6] Officials in Williston informed functionaries in Washington, D.C., that the letters had been returned. Three months later, on May 20, the

Department of Interior General Land Office in Washington replied with their form letter "C" dismissing the case, meaning that the corrections applied for were never made. The Williston office then sent Thor's and Anne's applications to Washington for filing.

Both Thor and Anne later claimed in sworn documents sent to the commissioner of the Land Office that they learned on June 2, 1907, that their applications to amend had been accepted. Consequently, on June 7, they journeyed to Williston by wagon and train and appeared in the Land Office to pursue the next step. An understanding must have been reached, because on that date, three years to the day from when they had first applied for their homesteads in Minot, Victor Schaffer, receiver in the Land Office in Williston, wrote a letter to the commissioner of the Washington Land Office with a request that the case be reopened. On October 12, 1907, four months after the first application to reopen the case, the Land Office in Washington, D.C. notified the register and receiver at the Williston Land Office that the amendment to reopen had been approved. The Williston office returned the amended application to the General Land Office on December 14, 1907. After two years of back-and-forth within the bureaucracy, the way was now cleared to set the record straight and transpose the Es and Ws. The moment for Thor and Anne to get their land free seemed finally to have arrived.[7]

Thor and Gjertru did not, however, receive their land for free. Instead they bought it outright from the government of the United States. Ironically enough, Thor and Gjertru did this because they desperately needed money. Four years after arriving on the prairie, they were homeless again. Their sod house had been gutted by fire on Easter morning. In order to pay for the lumber needed to construct a house, Thor and Gjertru made a compact with C. L. Dempster. If he would loan them $600, they would buy their land and immediately give Dempster a mortgage.

The Thor Birkelo house built in 1908, after their first house collapsed by fire, being examined by two Birkelo daughters, Gudrun Svendsbye and Margaret Nelson.

They would use one-third of the loan to buy the land and use the rest of the money to buy the lumber to build a frame house, as well as to pay for other needed items.

To replace the sod house, Thor built a three-room frame house. The center of the house was a two-story section about fourteen-by-twenty feet, adjoined to a single-story section that was about eight-by-sixteen. The house provided a kitchen and living room on the ground floor and sleeping quarters for the children upstairs. The small house occasioned the first of several mortgages. Between the spring of 1908 and the summer of 1914, Thor and Gjertru borrowed several thousand dollars and mortgaged the homestead at least eight times. Thor seems to have borrowed money both to pay previous debts and meet current needs. Thus he went further and further into debt as time passed. And interest rates were high, often ten percent.

Despite his bank loans, Thor continued to depend on his brother for assistance. Kristen paid Thor's real estate taxes at least three times. He paid $5.50 for 1906 taxes, $13.90 for 1907 taxes, and $11.12 for 1908 taxes. He even paid a $10.00 filing fee on June 27, 1907, when Thor was amending his homestead application, because Thor and Gjertru were strapped for ready cash.

Meanwhile, Thor's sister Anne died. The most complete picture we have of her is provided by her brother, Kristen, when he filed Final Proof testimony for her in the Williston Land Office. He stated that the "claimant was very poor," that she owned two cows, one heifer, two calves, and a few chickens and that she "would cut from ten to twelve loads of hay on the claim each year." He further testified that "she made her living on the claim by making and selling butter and doing knitting work, which work she would do on the claim and send away to sell." Additionally, he said she had about one-quarter of an acre "in garden each year, on which she raised potatoes and vegetables."[8] She also baked bread, which she sold to bachelor homesteaders, because every penny counted.

Anne died July 24, 1908, in Williston. In her will, which she wrote in Norwegian two days before she died, she gave instructions about how her property was to be distributed "in case my sickness and operation end in death."[9] There is no official record of her death or its cause. In her will, she stated that her doctor and the Williston hospital bills should be paid first. Anne was attended by Dr. Nels Myklestad, a native of Bergen, Norway, who had received his medical education at the University of Christiania

(Oslo). Dr. Myklestad paid the $94 burial costs for Anne at the George M. Thomas Funeral Home in Williston. This was not unusual for poverty cases, and physicians often tried later to collect these costs from family members. Anne's address on the funeral bill is given as Portland, Oregon. She did not live there, but her brother Kristen was living in Vancouver, Washington, just across the river from Portland. Because he handled her estate, it is reasonable to assume that the Portland address was intended as a reference to him and that he repaid Dr. Myklestad. The casket cost $50. Digging the grave was $5. Embalming cost $15. Anne was buried in a new dress that the funeral home bought for $13.

Anders Svendsbye Finds Farm and Family

After choosing his land in 1904, Anders Svendsbye spent a winter working as a lumberjack before returning to North Dakota in May of 1905 to build his house and begin clearing his land. He followed the same seasonal work pattern until the spring of 1907 when he returned to live and work that land for the better part of fifty years.

Anders' land was described in one Land Office document as "rolling prairie . . . no timber." It rolled gently to the south. It was very rocky and there were no trees, but it had other advantages. Among them was a deep slough. It produced excellent crops of hay and was a good source for water in the spring and early summer. The house Anders built had one window and one door. The window faced south and the door east. There were no openings to

The 10-foot by 12-foot homestead shack of Anders Svendsbye built in May 1905 and currently standing on the Svendsbye farm now owned by a Svendsbye grandson, Kenneth Vatne.

the west and north, from which the wind most often blew. The frame structure had only a single layer of exterior siding for walls. There was room inside for a stove, a bed, a table, and a couple of chairs, as well as a place for his trunk and some storage space for clothes and kitchen utensils. In addition to the house, Anders built a frame barn that was sixteen feet square and an eight-by-sixteen-foot frame granary. He dug a fourteen-foot well and bought a team of horses. By April 1910, he had broken forty-five acres of land and had cleared stones from an additional sixty acres. He valued his land between $900 and $1,000.

Acquiring the land was not altogether simple. In the final part of the process, Anders had to have neighbors verify that he had done to the land what was required by law and that he had lived on it for the prescribed length of time. He also had to release to the federal government all rights to any coal that might be under his land. Accordingly, on March 21, 1910, four neighbors gave testimony that Anders had resided on his homestead, broken his land, built his house, and dug his well. When asked how often the neighbors had seen Anders living on his claim, Martin Larson, who lived one-half mile west of Anders, testified "pretty near every day." On October 3, Samuel Adams, registrar in the Williston Land Office, wrote: "We have the honor to transmit herewith Anders A. Svendsbye's election to accept surface title."[10] The land was now his.

The year 1910 was a milestone year for Anders for another reason. On April 5, before A. H. Brown, clerk of the state's Eighth District Court in Williston, he became a citizen of the United States at a special session of the court. The Certificate of Naturalization reads, in part:

> Anders A. Svendsbye . . . of Temple . . . North Dakota having applied to be admitted a citizen of the United States of America, pursuant to law, and the court having found that the petitioner had resided continuously within the United States for at least five years and in this state for one year immediately preceding the date of the hearing of his petition, and that said petitioner intends to reside permanently in the United States, had in all respects complied with the law in relation thereto, and that he is entitled to be so admitted, it was thereupon ordered in the said court that he be admitted as a citizen of the United States of America.[11]

Thus, by the end of 1910, Anders Svendsbye had become a citizen of the United States and had secured title to a farm.

Two years later the landowner and citizen married Lina Hove (Hovemoen). Born in Hundorp, Gudbrandsdal, Norway, on November 12, 1876, Lina left Oslo alone at the age of twenty-six on the liner Tunrain, arriving in Detroit on July 28, 1903. Her brother Ole had arrived in the United States a year earlier and lived in Devils Lake, North Dakota; this may have beckoned her to North Dakota. In any case, on July 23, 1907, Lina appeared in the district court in Williston to file her Declaration of

Intent to become a U.S. citizen. She, too, decided to homestead and did so on eighty acres in the southeast corner of Section 1 of Township 159 North, 96 Range West, one and one-half miles east of Ole's homestead.

On October 30, 1908, she bought her land for $100 or $1.25 per acre, which is recorded as payment in full for the land. While she saw to her own farming or rented her land to others, Lina found other work as well. According to the 1910 U.S. Census, she was working as a maid (the census used "servant") for the Edward and Otillia Iverson family, who lived about two miles west of her homestead.

There is no record of how Anders Svendsbye and Lina Hove met or how they may have courted, but on July 22, 1912, they went together to Williston, accompanied by their attendants Dora Strand and Ole Hove, and there they were married by Pastor Albert Johansen. On their marriage license application, Anders gave his address as Temple and Lina hers as Harry, the first name of the community that later became Hamlet. It appears that Anders and Lina spent most of the first year of their marriage in the ten-by-twelve-foot house Anders had built on his homestead. In the spring of the following year, their neighbors, Ingeborg and Bernhard Roll, decided to sell their land and

Anders Svendsbye and Lina Hove on their wedding day, July 22, 1912.

leave for Canada. Consequently, on March 12, 1913, Anders and Lina bought 160 acres from the Roll family, who had homesteaded adjacent to Anders. They paid $3,200 for the land.

The Rolls had built a small house that provided more living space and the young couple made this their own. The main part of the house was a two-story structure, about fourteen by twenty feet. To that was attached the homestead unit built by the Rolls, which served as their kitchen. When attached to the two-story structure, it provided a three-room house. The foundation was unmortared stones positioned on the ground.

During these first years of marriage, Anders apparently did the shopping for groceries at Simon-Berg in McGregor and left several slips which tell something about the style of life they lived. On April 3, 1913, he bought oranges for 30 cents and a pair of gloves for $2. He also purchased soap for 25 cents, coffee for $1.50, pickles for 30 cents, and paper napkins for 5 cents. In 1905, coffee in Tioga sold for 14 cents per pound. On April 11, he purchased tooth-picks for 5 cents, salt for 20 cents, yeast for 10 cents, and corn flakes, corn starch, matches, catsup, and Jello for 25 cents each. He bought shoes for $5 and paid 40 cents for flower and vegetable seeds. On June 6, he bought an overall for $1. Peas, baking powder, and seed onions cost 25 cents each. Rutabagas cost only 10 cents, whereas tomatoes were $3.50, salt 30 cents, and lemons 70 cents. On June 17, he brought home syrup for 25 cents and a plow share for $3.25. On August 11, he bought crackers, chocolate, and oatmeal for 25 cents each and beans for 50 cents. He procured lemons for 40 cents, onions for 25 cents, a shirt for $2.00, hooks for 5 cents, and a pair of pants for $7. He also sold butter. In 1915, he sold fifteen pounds of butter to Simon-Berg for 20 cents per pound. By 1921, the price for a pound of butter had risen to 30 cents per pound.

A year after doubling the size of their land and moving into a larger house, their first child was born on their farm. Writing to his brother Elling in Norway, Anders reported, "We have gotten a little daughter" who was "in the best of health."[12] Born on May 10, 1914, she was named Margaret. Another child had been stillborn, perhaps in 1913. Then, only three years after their marriage, Lina developed cancer of the stomach. Dr. Robert Stobie of Tioga first performed surgery on Lina on the kitchen table. Gjertru Birkelo assisted him. Anders held the kitchen lamp to give Dr. Stobie additional light. In spite of these efforts, Lina died on June 21 at 7:00 p.m. She was buried in Grong Cemetery, one and one-half miles east of where she and Anders lived. She was laid to rest beside her stillborn child. One month before her death, Lina had sold her land to N. P. Nelson of Hamlet for $1,000, at the same time paying off the $500 mortgage.

To keep Margaret in his home and provide some kind of motherly presence for her, Anders invited his brother Elling and his wife, Johanna, to live with him. Elling and Johanna had returned just a few months earlier from their honeymoon in Norway. One month after Lina's death, Johanna gave birth to her and Elling's first child, Bertha Marie. How long the living arrangement with Elling and Johanna lasted is not certain. A second child,

Albert Johan, was born to them in 1917, and a third, Leonard Oliver, in 1918. With their own children to care for, it seems reasonable that their mutual living arrangement could not have lasted more than two years, likely less. After Elling and Johanna returned to their farm, Gjertru and Thor Birkelo looked after Margaret. Often Thor and Gjertru's daughter, Gudrun, had charge of the little girl.

On December 5, 1918, Anders and Gudrun were married. They drove to Wildrose in Anders' new Dort automobile and were married in the Lutheran parsonage of Pastor Mathias Jacobson Berge, who was living in Wildrose while serving congregations of the Norwegian Lutheran Church in America in that area. Their wedding attendants were Sigurd Birkelo and Hannah Larson, both of Hamlet. Gudrun was seventeen years old. She was a petite, kind, and gracious young woman. In order to permit her to marry before coming of legal age, her father had signed an X on a document before Judge A. L. Butler of the Williams County Court.

Gudrun Birkelo had been born on September 19, 1901, in the town of Levanger, about thirty-five miles north of Trondheim. She was baptized in the church at Levanger on November 10, with five sponsors, one of whom was her oldest sister, Synnove (Sena). Gudrun recalled nothing about crossing the Atlantic with her mother and five siblings in the spring of 1905. After arriving in the United States, she attended the Hankey School, two miles south from where she lived, and later worked in a variety of homes in the Hamlet community until her marriage to Anders.

CHAPTER 3

Connections and Communities

The Railroads

Railroads were crucial in the settlement of the Upper Midwest. For the people living in the northernmost part of North Dakota, the most important railroad was the Great Northern. It was the railroad that brought the Svendsbye and Birkelo families to northwestern North Dakota, along with almost everyone else who settled there. The person who almost single-handedly brought that railroad into existence was a one-eyed Canadian dropout from a Quaker academy named James J. Hill. He out-maneuvered every potential contender because of his native intelligence, leadership, and organizational skills. In 1878 he persuaded three fellow Canadians, including the president of the Bank of Montreal, to negotiate a contract with $280,000 in earnest money to purchase a small railroad which by 1890 had been expanded and given the name Great Northern. Three years later, that railroad—the only one built without land grants from the federal government—stretched to Seattle, attaining Hill's goal of reaching the Pacific Ocean so that he could start trading with the Orient, and giving northern North Dakotans a world market. Achieving that goal involved laying track from Minnesota starting in 1879 and reaching the West Coast in 1893.

The railroad had arrived in Williston on October 6, 1887. In the spring of that year, 8,000 men and 6,000 horses were involved in grading the roadbed, requiring 16,000 carloads of lumber, rails, and spikes delivered on time for just that year's operations, as well as 600,000 bushels of oats to feed the horses. Hidy, Hidy, Scott, and Hofsommer describe the operation this way:

> Track-laying was a raucous symphony of men and horses, ringing iron, and hammering blows. Hordes of men moved mountains of ties from the construction train to massed wagons, whence they were hauled to the graded roadbed, unto

which ties were unloaded and precisely spaced, rails were hauled on low iron cars from Minot to the end-of-track. Burly workers hoisted unto ties; others distributed angle bars, bolts and spikes; finally came the spikers.[1]

The transformation in transportation brought about by the railroad came to the area where Anders and the Birkelos lived in 1911. That year construction was completed on a part of a Great Northern "spur" running west and somewhat north from Stanley. The spur branched off its main line half-way between Minot and Williston, and ran as far as seven miles west of what became Hamlet to what would become the town of Wildrose. With the completion of the spur to the end of the line near the Montana border in 1916, the railroad ushered in the establishment of many towns and villages about every seven or eight miles along its route. The reason for that distance was that four miles, the halfway point between the towns, was considered the desirable distance for farmers to haul their grain to market with horses. With the railroad's extension west from Powers Lake in 1911, four towns sprang up: Battle View, McGregor, Hamlet and Wildrose. Five years later, the Great Northern spur had been built as far as was planned. The end-of-the-line town was named Grenora (an abbreviation for Great Northern Railway). Between the towns of Wildrose and Grenora, five more towns sprang up: Corinth, Alamo, Zahl, Appam, and Hanks.

The reason for locating towns next to the railroad was commercial. The railroad transported goods to and from the new towns. Beginning in 1911, the train made one round trip along the spur, leaving Stanley one day and returning the next. Coal, lumber, hay, food, and clothing came into the towns, and grain, milk, and cream were regularly shipped out. On special occasions, cattle, hogs, and sheep were shipped to St. Paul, Minnesota, for slaughter. Gradually, the Great Northern increased its runs until it made the trip from Stanley to Grenora and back on a daily basis. Going west, it left Stanley in the evening, traveling overnight to Grenora, and returning to Stanley the next day. On May 10, 1912, a passenger car was added to the end of the train, providing transportation from town to town for half a century.

The New Towns

Hamlet was located near the middle of the spur line between Stanley and Grenora. The town did a little dance before it was given a permanent location and name. At first it was located approximately in the same spot it occupies today in Section 2 of Big Meadow Township, right next to the railroad. It was called Hankey, for Frank D. Hankey, the first pioneer to settle in what became Big Meadow Township. He had opened the area's first post office in 1910 on his Lazy K Ranch and named it for himself as the first postmaster. When the town Hankey was formed, the post office moved there from the Lazy K Ranch. A year and a half later, Edward Battleson relocated the post office about two miles southwest of Hankey and called it Harry for one of his sons. But on April 19, 1913, the post office was returned to Hankey, and Postmaster Edward Battleson renamed the town Hamlet, from the French word *hamelet* meaning "a small village." The post office was the immigrants' connecting point to the world outside, distributing not only letters, but also newspapers in both English and foreign languages brought to town each day by the Great Northern. Until telephones were installed, news entered homes and communities only via the print media and letters brought by the railway—one of its most important functions in a pioneer community.

The Battleson brothers—Edward and Andrew—were to Hamlet what Nels Simon was to Tioga. They were involved in the opening of a general merchandise store in 1911, changing its name to Hamlet Mercantile in 1913 when they became the sole owners. It was located on a corner looking east directly across the street from where Kenneth and Shirley Vatne now live. The Battlesons also owned the Dort Automobile Agency and the Hamlet Implement and Hardware Company. A bank, with Frank McCoy as cashier, opened just south of the Hamlet Mercantile, across the street, east of where the livery barn stood. In 1923, the bank was moved to Wildrose. The town grew as two blacksmith shops, a billiard parlor and barbershop, two restaurants, a rooming house, a second grocery store, a lumber yard along the south side of the railroad, a livery stable, a grain elevator, and two Lutheran churches were added. From March 18 to June 18, 1914, the *Hamlet Times* was published weekly on the back page of the *McGregor Herald*. The grain elevator, established in 1911 as the Nelson Grain Company, is the longest and only surviving Hamlet enterprise.

In addition to these businesses, there were some important civic groups. For about ten years, Hamlet had a six-person orchestra that advertised itself as "The Finest Musical Troupe in the Northwest." They gave regular concerts of classical music in Hamlet Hall and played for dances. Hamlet also boasted a fifty-member band that was invited to play at the Northwest Fair in Minot in 1927 to honor Roald Amundson and Lincoln Elsworth following their trip to the North Pole. Bernt Strand was the musical director, Andrew Battleson president, and A. C. Hankey secretary-treasurer. In 1930 the town had a population of 219. That dropped to twenty-five some thirty years later; by 2008 it was down to six people.

The other two towns that became important to the lives of Anders and Gudrun Svendsbye were McGregor and Wildrose. In the case of both towns, mail service was started before either town was established. It was started in the Wildrose area first by Edward O. Salveson on his homestead in Section 25 in what became Hazel Township, just west of the future Big Meadow. It had mail deliveries twice a week and was known as the Stordahl Post Office. In July 1906, after the U. S. Post Office approved her appointment, Mrs. Anna E. Palmer established a post office in her kitchen on her homestead north of the present Wildrose site and later named Montrose. She was succeeded by S. A. Padden, who changed the name to Paddington. That held until the railroad came in November 1911 when all eleven businesses in Paddington moved south to the Nels Akre farm next to the railroad, and the Great Northern re-named the place Wildrose.

The town grew quickly, numbering forty families only one year later. Horses and wagons were used to distribute goods from the railroad to the stores. Four grain elevators were immediately constructed, and Wildrose claimed itself as "the nation's largest primary grain market in the world" until 1916 when the spur reached Grenora. Some farmers required four days to deliver one wagon box of grain to the elevator and return home. To accommodate all the grain haulers, Wildrose had three hotels and three livery barns, followed by three lumber yards, three banks, two hardware stores with funeral parlors, a newspaper, an International Harvester dealership, a photo shop, a jewelry store, a drug store, a blacksmith shop, and four grocery stores. Two churches quickly sprang up. In 1918, one could buy tailor-made suits for $18, $20, and $25. One cafe had so much business that its owner had to hire two women to assist him. The pastry cook, Mrs. Emma Redal, baked fifty to sixty pies daily. Haircuts in 1917 cost 40 cents and shaves, 20 cents. A busy blacksmith shop sharpened plow shares and shoed horses for 25 cents each hoof.

Similar developments occurred at the site of what became McGregor. The post office was opened in the John J. Lynch home, the site of the future town, perhaps as early as 1904, with Alice Lynch as postmaster. The mail came by train to Tioga and from there by horses to the Lynch home three times a week. The town was named for William McGregor, a leader of the immigrant community who came from Canada via St.

Cloud. He was the first chairman of both the Sauk Valley Township Board and the Sauk Valley School Board, and was postmaster for three years before McGregor was organized in June of 1910. Construction of the town began before the coming of the railroad so wagons from the McGregor Ranch hauled grain over a "rutted ungraded trail"to Tioga and returned with lumber from the Dixon Lumber Company. S. E. Spangrud built a hardware store in 1910 and gained the reputation for selling the first goods over the counter in McGregor to customer C. O. Melander. Several other businesses followed to meet the needs of the settlers. Ole Hanson hired Emil Forsgren and his son Evald to haul a store building across the prairie with their steam engine to the main street of McGregor to serve as the first general store in town. Next came a second general store, a bank, a meat market, a drugstore, a pool hall, a blacksmith shop, a feed grinding mill and garage, dray line services, a lumber yard, two grain elevators, and a newspaper. The school building was moved to town from the Geiger farm where it had been built. A Lutheran congregation was formed and met in homes for several years before a building was secured. Most of these developments occurred within a decade as the town of McGregor was launched.

The coming of the railroad in 1911 changed and simplified life considerably for farmers like Anders Svendsbye. Previously, they had to haul their grain, usually hard spring wheat, to Temple, Tioga, or Ray, using horses to pull a wagon with a box that held between fifty and sixty bushels. That trip normally required two days, especially if the farmer had additional tasks to perform—visiting the bank or the machinery dealer, or getting a haircut. Because the distances were so great, farmers helped one another by shopping for their neighbors. Flour, salt, and coffee were almost always needed staples. Now, along with the advance of the railroad, new towns were springing up only a few miles from where the farmers lived. Moreover, the trains would transport their grain from the new towns to milling centers; at the local elevator they could get their grain to market in a few hours instead of one or two days. Shopping for groceries and other necessities, including machinery, was made easier for people living on the prairie.

The road system was slow to develop. Initially, farmers traveled to Tioga or Ray using the shortest possible route across the prairie, forming trails easily followed before the snow covered them. Those prairie trails dotted the countryside and were used year after year as the homesteaders went from town to town and neighbor to neighbor by horse-drawn wagons.

As the first important town for the Svendsbye and Birkelo families, Tioga had ample livery barn space so that when farmers got to town, they could, for a fee, put their horses in the barn, water them, and feed them hay and oats. Some farmers may have rented a hotel room to stay overnight. Others, at least in warmer weather, slept in the haymow of the livery barn. In the evening, the bar—and later two bars—did good business as the farmers, after their evening meal in a local restaurant, drank their beer or whiskey, played cards, told stories, and visited.[2] In the process, friendships developed among individuals and communities.

While the homesteaders were busy converting the prairie into fields that produced a wide variety of small grains such as wheat, oats, barley, rye, and flax, they continued to confront an environment that had two fierce opponents: snow and fire. The communities abounded with stories about fierce blizzards, some that brought so much snow that it covered both house and barn, requiring owners to break a window to get out of the house. Water had to be lowered to the animals through a hole in the barn roof. The settlers sometimes tied twine around their waists and to the houses and barns to find their way between buildings. Early on, there were no telephones so one had to wait and wonder what had happened when some family member(s) got caught in a storm and could not get home. In general, families relied on the good will of other settlers to welcome anyone caught in a storm to stay at their homestead, where both humans and horses were given food and shelter until the winds and the snows ceased.

Anders recalled a snowstorm that came up suddenly as he was traveling home from Tioga. It was snowing and blowing so furiously that he could not see where to go. He tied the leather reins, used to direct the horses, to the wagon box, turned his back to the wind, and let the horses find their way back to the farm. When the horses—likely Frank and Fanny—stopped a few hours later, their heads were touching the corner of the house on Anders' homestead. His was not a unique experience. Other neighbors told similar stories. The North Dakota prairie was a strange world in which horses saved people's lives.

There were fewer fires than snow storms, but the worst ones were equally devastating. The settlers burned large spaces around their buildings and haystacks to detour the fire around them. Carl Salveson, caught by a fire while traveling home, had to start a fire ahead of him so he could drive his horses onto the burned prairie just as the main fire was about to overtake him. In 1904, fire burned a path 400 miles wide in western North Dakota and eastern Montana, forcing at least one family to use wetted-down bedding to protect a stack of flax.

Those hardships were generally taken in stride by the homesteaders. The weather, cold or hot, together with an occasional fire, were simply a part of the context in which their work was done. The weather in Norway and Sweden had been cold in the winter, sometimes bringing several feet of snow. The immigrants were accustomed to dressing warmly and toughing it out. They may have been surprised that sometimes the temperatures on the prairie were higher in the summer and lower in the winter than in Scandinavia. But although the weather was the subject for much conversation, there was little real complaint.

Communication, Electrical and Medical Developments

New developments in the agricultural industry soon appeared on the prairie. These developments were the advent of steam and gasoline power to replace horse power. Coinciding with the advent of steam and gasoline power was the arrival in the pioneer community of two more radically transforming agents: a new communications system—the telephone—and a new power system—electricity. These developments revolutionized life in ways undreamed of when the first immigrants had arrived only a few years earlier. The Williston paper reported in the fall of 1905 that

> a gang of men are working on the Great Northern telephone line from here west and it is expected that the line will be completed this far in a few days. A gang is also working this way from Minot and it is said that the two gangs will meet at Ross or White Earth. This line, when completed will give us telephone connections with all points between Minot and Williston.[3]

Tioga's telephone company was organized two years later. On June 8, 1908, Tioga Township granted a franchise to the Tioga and Farmers Telephone Company, authorizing the construction of lines in the township and the village of Tioga. A few years later, an office and switchboard opened in McGregor, which served the area south and east of Hamlet. The Wildrose community purchased their system from the Noonan Telephone Company for $2,750 in 1915 and named it the Wildrose Mutual Telephone Company. Elmer Noyes came from Minnesota to Wildrose in 1914 to construct the lines and to install the phones and switchboard.

Tioga main street.

Anders Svendsbye had a telephone installed in his home as soon as one was available, near the beginning of World War I. There were no private lines. Several farms shared an extension. Each farm was assigned a different code to indicate who was being called. The Svendsbyes' was one long ring and one short. One memorized the codes for neighbors as well as one's own. When they heard the telephone ring, everyone on that extension knew who was receiving a telephone call and could listen to the conversation simply by lifting the receiver to their ear. Listening to neighbors' calls was a form of entertainment as well as a means to inform the community what was happening in the lives of their neighbors. If person X living in Minot called person Y living near Hamlet, both the simple fact of the call and details of its contents had the potential for becoming known throughout the community. People with telephones listened in on conversations—it was called "rubbernecking"—and repeated the contents around the family dinner table. The information later was shared with neighbors, often over a cup of coffee.

Families could directly call others on their extension. But to call someone in a neighboring community or to call long distance, people had to call through a switchboard with an operator in the employ of the telephone company. The Svendsbye phone was connected to the McGregor switchboard. Tioga and Wildrose each had a telephone office with switchboard. Those telephone systems served the communities for nearly half a century. The Northwest Communications Cooperative, based in Ray, was established in 1965. It took over all the phone companies in the county and laid many of the lines underground, protecting them from snow and ice storms. Not until then were private lines installed in nearly all homes and businesses, providing people in the area the kind of phone service common in most of the nation.

Electricity came to the prairie about the same time as the telephones, but it took much longer to arrive at most farms. Williston had electricity as early as 1907. According to the Williams County history, Wildrose was "one of the first towns in North Dakota to have electric lights." It celebrated the arrival of electricity in about 1913 when Harry Lomen and Fred Fortier built and operated an electric plant. Apparently there were complaints about the noise from the exhaust of the two engines. "When these engines begin to snort, they shake the windows in the nearby houses and make things very disagreeable." Despite complaints, use of electricity was so extensive that in 1915, Fortier announced the need for another engine and dynamo. This notice appeared in the August 13, 1925, Wildrose newspaper:

> Beginning at once the light plant will be run from 8 to 11:30 a.m. for ironing Tuesdays. . . . Beginning August 15 the lights will be on all night; business men are requested to leave one light burning all night inside and also one or two lights outside as needed.[4]

In 1914, Tioga began operating a light plant known as the Tioga Electric Company. According to the county history, it was powered at first by "a 25 horse power kerosene engine running a 16 kilowatt generator which produced a direct current running from 110 and 130 watts." The plant operated until midnight. At 11:45 p.m. the lights would blink several times to warn the customers that the electricity would be off in fifteen minutes. "On Monday the plant would operate until noon, so that washing machines could be operated."

Ultimately, electric service was taken over by Montana Dakota Utilities Company. It built power lines to all the towns in the county. Electricity likely was available to persons living in all towns in the county by at least 1920. Some farmers installed wind and gasoline-powered generators. The 1923–1924 edition of the Williams County Directory carried an advertisement from Foss and Astrup of Grenora for Delco light plants for individual farms. But the amount of electricity generated in that fashion was limited. Full-time, affordable electric power came to most rural residents, including Anders' farm, only in 1949 when the Rural Electric

Administration (REA), financed by the federal government, built power lines in Williams County.

Medical care came to the area early and was delivered in one way that the twenty-first century cannot match—directly into the home. The first doctors serving the Hamlet area lived in Tioga and Wildrose. They drove their horses in good weather and bad to reach their patients on farms. Prior to the coming of the telephone, they had to be summoned in person. The distance from the Svendsbye farm to Tioga was a good day's journey with horses. Before the day of the automobile, it would have taken two days to bring a doctor to the patient's bedside. The doctors apparently left their offices at a moment's notice to help those who were sick, and they performed surgery under the most primitive circumstances.

> Dr. Robert Stobie came to Tioga in the fall of 1906 as its first doctor, and a pharmacy was opened that same year. According to the Williams County history, Stobie "performed more than one emergency operation on a kitchen table in a farm house."

Lina Svendsbye, Anders' first wife, was one of those people. On Lina's death certificate, Stobie says he attended Lina from June 18 to June 21, 1915. By that time, he likely owned an automobile, because in 1909 Henry Ford was selling his assembly-line-constructed touring Model T Ford for $850.

The Wildrose community got its first doctor in 1910, but he only stayed until 1915. That same year Dr. R. K. Sarheim, a native of Stavanger, Norway, and a graduate of the University of Illinois, established a medical practice in Wildrose that lasted until his death in 1922. During his seven years in the area, he called on people between Alamo and McGregor, traveling with horses before he acquired an automobile. Sometimes he even traveled on the railroad tracks using a "speeder," a four-wheeled vehicle that was manually propelled on the tracks. Like his predecessors in the neighboring communities, he performed surgery on the kitchen table and battled snowstorms to reach patients' homes. He was succeeded by Dr. Carl August Wicklund, who was followed by Dr. E. W. Zeiss. Both continued the practice of calling on people in their homes rather than requiring the sick to come to their offices.

The Wildrose community got another important medical personage in 1919 with the arrival of Sigrid Andersen, who was a sister of Dr. Sarheim's wife, Caspara. Sigrid, and her husband, Carl, were important members of the community for some twenty years, until they moved to Brooklyn, New York, during World War II. Sigrid, a nurse, started a hospital on the upper floor of a building on the west side of the north end of Main Street. There she maintained four rooms as the Wildrose Hospital. "Nurse Andersen," as she was called, worked with three doctors in succession until the last one left in the late 1930s. Then she operated the hospital by herself. In 1934 she delivered Gudrun Svendsbye's eighth child, Edward. She cared for Gjertru Birkelo at the time of her death on January 8, 1939. She did miscellaneous tasks, such as carefully fitting together two pieces of the tip of a finger that had nearly been severed when one of the Svendsbye children was using a small ax to split a piece of wood he had been holding between his left thumb and forefinger.

Dr. Robert Goodman, who came to Powers Lake in 1930, was especially appreciated by the residents of the Hamlet-McGregor community for the house calls he made to them through the 1930s, 1940s, and 1950s, battling snow, rain, and mud. He was the last of the old-fashioned country doctors who provided health care directly to the farmers on the prairie in northwestern North Dakota. A brusque man, he once came to the Svendsbye farm when Anders was ill and greeted the family as he came through the door with "He isn't dead yet, is he?"

The first dentist to come to Wildrose arrived in 1916 and stayed two and one-half years. Next was Dr. Horace Straight who served for nine years beginning in 1926. He extracted teeth without an anesthetic at a charge of $1 per tooth. He was succeeded by Dr. Lawrence Carlson who took care of several of the Svendsbye siblings, all of whom appreciated him very much. He performed extractions, took care of fillings, and did the variety of technical steps necessary to produce false teeth. My oldest brother, Albert paid the cost of the first fillings I needed. While one's jaw was often sore when some of the work was completed, Dr. Carlson nevertheless saved many a tooth, which, with additional care, have lasted my lifetime. The community was sad when he moved to Williston in 1945, but many people remained his faithful clients, traveling to his Williston office. He was the last medical professional in Wildrose.

The one and only veterinarian, Dr. W. J. Hayes, worked in Wildrose during World War I. That was a medical service Anders deemed unnecessary. The calves were all de-horned by Albert. For some reason, the cattle never became ill and suffered only such things as a growth which was treated with some home remedy usually purchased at a hardware store.

Perhaps more importantly, the cattle were never allowed to get old. They were sold for beef to the local cattle buyer while they were still reasonably young. Horses, on the other hand, were never sold but remained on the farm until they died of old age or had to be shot for some malady. One painful and sad experience occurred in the summer of 1940. The previous fall, Anders and Albert had bought a beautiful white gelding named Dick for $35. Nervous and fast in all his movements, he quickly became a favorite of Albert's. One day while lying in his stall, he threw his back out when trying to get up. He tried and tried but could never get to his feet. There was no conversation about whether a veterinarian should be called. Maybe that was thought to be unaffordable. After a few days, Dick died. Albert was devastated. Decades later, when Albert developed a herd of beautiful Herefords, he regularly called the vet from Powers Lake to come to the farm to vaccinate the animals and to perform other services whenever the cattle needed such attention.

While a few physicians, like Dr. Goodman of Powers Lake, continued to make house calls until he retired, most doctors quit doing that some time between the two world wars. The only option people had then was to visit a doctor's office and, when necessary, be hospitalized. Williston, which had been incorporated in 1894, got its first hospital in 1905 when Dr. L. R. Dochterman started the Frances Hospital in a private home and had it converted into a hospital. It was superseded by two other hospitals, the Good Samaritan and Mercy. The Good Samaritan Hospital was started in 1912 when the Rev. Albert Johnson, pastor of United Norwegian Lutheran Church, organized efforts to establish Wittenberg Hospital. It, too, began in a family dwelling that, together with two smaller buildings, was converted into hospital space. In 1929, construction of Good Samaritan was completed as the successor to Wittenberg and, for all practical purposes, was a Lutheran hospital. A Roman Catholic hospital, known as Mercy, was started in 1920 by Dr. E. J. Hagen when he, Father Edward O'Neill, and W. S. Davidson Sr. invited the Sisters of Mercy to come to Williston to provide nursing staff. The Sisters purchased an apartment building for $61,000 and converted it into hospital space, which, over the years, was greatly expanded. Later, the two hospitals merged using the name Mercy, enlarged the span of coverage, and became an important medical center in western North Dakota. Tioga was in the hospital business for only a short time, having acquired a two-story house in 1910 that closed rather quickly. Powers Lake, on the other hand, worked hard to support Dr. Robert Goodman and completed construction of a hospital in 1937 that served the area until it closed in 1970.

Another important medical development in Williams County was a public health nursing program established in the early 1930s. It focused primarily on the rural and elementary schools which the "county nurse," as she was called, regularly visited. She tested students for vision, inspected their teeth, reviewed their nutrition, and observed their cleanliness. One of the most important ventures began in 1943 when she started immunization clinics for diphtheria and smallpox, later adding whooping cough, tetanus, and ultimately polio.

Building Roads

One of the developments late in coming was the building of good roads, despite the fact that roads were one of the first concerns of the pioneer township boards. Early construction focused on connecting the county's towns, following the section lines which the legislature in 1899 had designated for use as public roads. But they were dirt roads that were difficult to use when it rained or snowed. To be sure, the road situation in North Dakota was not very different from that across much of the nation. One of the factors pressing both national and state governments to facilitate interstate travel was the increase in the number of cars and trucks on those roads. In 1904, there were only 205 miles of gravel graded road in the entire state. North Dakota had a long way to go. By the end of World War I, there were still no hard-surfaced roads. But considerable progress was made by the end of the next decade. By 1928, according to Elwyn Robinson, "There was a state highway system of 7,200 miles; about 4,000 miles of it had been graded and 2,400 miles given a gravel surface." Still, by 1927, there were only ten miles paved in the entire state.

These facts were terribly important to the Svendsbye family and all citizens of North Dakota. Most people today have never had the experience of getting a vehicle stuck in the mud and therefore cannot imagine what that was like. The road that ran past the Svendsbye farm was hazardous at a point just beyond the tree field. After heavy rains or during the spring thaw, it was nearly impossible to drive across a spot about 200 feet long without getting stuck. It was not uncommon for strangers to walk to the Svendsbye house, knock on the door, and ask Anders or Albert if they would pull them out of the mud. At such times Albert or Anders regularly harnessed a team of their strongest horses to successfully get that job done, gratis. Neither of them complained about being asked, but they did talk about how difficult it sometimes was to pull some vehicles to a drier spot on the road. At times, not only horses were required, but planks and gravel as well, with humans pushing. Those experiences were not unique to the Svendsbyes. Hence, people living in North Dakota were concerned about the condition of the roads and watched the newspapers closely to see what the state legislature and county commissioners might do to improve them. Appropriations for road construction were important.

There was a sense that bad roads held people hostage. This was the case for the Svendsbye family in the winter of 1932 when Lillian had an attack of acute appendicitis. The closest hospital was in Williston, but car travel was out because the roads were blocked with snow. The only way to a doctor was by train. But snow-blocked roads nearly killed that idea, too. Anders had to use horses and a sleigh to take Lillian and Gudrun to Hamlet where they waited for the morning train to take them to Stanley. That train did not get them there in time to catch the west-bound train to Williston, so they had to wait to catch the east-bound train to Minot, since there was only one train a day in each direction. By the time Lillian got to Trinity Hospital in Minot, her appendix had ruptured. It so poisoned her system that she had to be hospitalized for a month before she was well enough to go home. There was no health insurance at that time, so Anders worked at paying the hospital bill but had to let the doctor's bill ride. Soon the bill collector was writing Anders about the unpaid $150 doctor's bill. Such were the tensions that plagued families on the prairies. A child's life was at stake. No passable roads. Horses and trains to the rescue. No money available for either doctor or hospital. Efforts to pay the hospital still left the doctor's bill collector at the door.

It took four decades to get road improvements really going. One of the two east-west highways in the state was Highway #2 which extended from Houlton, Maine, to Everett, Washington. It ran about fifteen miles south of the Svendsbye farm, and they used it when they went to Williston. Upgrading of that road began in 1919 when some businessmen in Duluth met to plan a memorial to Theodore Roosevelt. Max Skidmore referred to it as "one of the prairie arteries that permitted America to move out of the mud." Williston pulled out all stops on May 23, 1942, to celebrate its completion. Five governors, headed by North Dakota's John Moses, twenty-one marching bands, several concerts, and two banquets were on the program for the day. It was an event so important the entire Svendsbye family joined the celebration. Four decades later, all the major county highways were hard-surfaced—a welcome development Anders and Gudrun never lived to see.

As one looks back, one can say that after the first three decades of life on the prairie, despite the quality of roads and the Depression, the settlers had witnessed enormous transformations. The prairie had been turned into productive farmland. Trains carried people, grain, food, and goods between communities and across the continent. New towns clustered along the railroad. Businesses, schools, churches, and hospitals rose up in the new communities. Some immigrants moved on, but many stayed until they were later driven away by dust storms. For most of the first three decades, however, life seemed to be working out in fulfillment of the dreams that had brought the immigrants across the Atlantic. The work was hard, but on the whole life was satisfying and enjoyable, and the people prospered.

CHAPTER 4

School and Church

Early Schools

As soon as the breaking of land began and homes were erected, arrangements for school classrooms and worship space were made in most North Dakota communities. The rapidity with which the newcomers established schools and churches suggests that their vision for a new and better life in the United States involved more than economic betterment. Their vision was not narrowly focused. It was comprehensive. It included the kind of culture they intended to establish. They envisioned a culture in which the people were well educated and free—even encouraged—to worship in their new environment. It was a vision shared by citizens across the nation and implemented from coast to coast with incredible speed.

All the towns in Williams County reflected that high commitment to education. Tioga, which was established in 1902, opened its first school that same year in space on the second floor of the Simon store. The town built its first school building two years later, and in 1908 they built a two-story brick structure that accommodated twelve grades. The town held its first high school graduation nine years later when they awarded diplomas to five students.

McGregor did not even exist when that area's first school opened with six students in 1905 in a sixteen-by-twenty homestead shack in Section 34 of Sauk Valley Township which the district rented for $1 a year from Marion Gillette. The following year, the district built its first school building on the Geiger farm southwest of the future town-site for a cost of $925. It was moved into McGregor in 1910, the year the town was established; the building was partitioned to create space for two classrooms and two teachers. Enrollment grew so rapidly that a four-room brick building was completed in 1919. The first McGregor high school graduation was celebrated two years later when two students graduated.

The Wildrose community story is similar. Before the town came into being, there were seven schools serving the area, three of which were in homestead shacks or granaries. The first opened in 1904 with six students in a granary on the Martin Walstad homestead in Section 24 on the eastern side of the future Hazel Township. When the city was formed in 1910, the Wildrose Special School District 90 was created, and a two-story structure was soon constructed in town to replace several temporary structures. Counting its antecedents, the school functioned for over a century before it closed in 2006 because of declining enrollment.

The first schools in the Hamlet area were two Hankey schools, one built in 1902 in Section 22, the other in 1903 in Section 23 of the future Big Meadow Township where the Hankey Ranch was located. It appears that the first school closed after one year. Thus, in the Hamlet community as in neighboring communities, construction of a school began before most of the homesteaders arrived on the prairie.

The Birkelos were among the families served by the Hankey School. The November 27, 1909, teacher's report to the Williams County superintendent lists the names of fifteen students enrolled, including Gudrun, Inga, and Theodore Birkelo. The records are not complete, so it is not clear when they first enrolled. They had arrived in the community in 1905 and may have been in attendance since that time. They were registered for courses in reading, writing, spelling, and arithmetic. In the June 1913 teacher's report, Inga and Theodore were no longer attending. In addition to the four courses listed two years earlier, Gudrun was studying language or grammar and physiology. Theodore was back in school for a term that ran from April 15 to June 30, 1914.

Gudrun was the only Birkelo enrolled for a term that ran from September 6 to December 23, 1915. It was likely her last. How many terms were offered each year and how many constituted an academic year is not clear. Hence we cannot be certain how many years of schooling Gudrun had nor how many grades she completed. Oral tradition tells us that she completed five grades. Her highest mark in her fifth year was in spelling, followed by reading and history. Other courses in which she was registered over the years were geography, agriculture, drawing, and penmanship.[1]

The attendance records of the school suggest an interesting story of a young girl on the prairie. Despite the fact she likely walked the two miles to school, she was never tardy. She was absent from two to eleven days during the school year, except for one year when the number was higher.

These absences may have been due to the fact she had to walk to school. Some days the weather would have been too cold or too stormy to manage the four miles required of her each day. Even so, she was absent less than her two older siblings.

However incomplete, the records contain several items of interest. The June 30, 1910, clerk's report states that the school had no well or cistern but that each student had a drinking cup. Water apparently was hauled from the well on the Hankey Ranch nearby. During the 1909-1910 academic year, the teacher was paid $45 per month and $32.70 was spent for text books. The 1914 report stated that there were nineteen volumes in the three Hankey School libraries. The number had grown to 150 volumes three years later. In 1919, reflecting patriotic concerns aroused during World War I, the county asked each of the schools to report if they had a US flag. Each of the Hankey schools did.

The Hamlet School

It is unclear when a school was started in Hamlet because the earliest minutes of the Hamlet school Board are missing. One school was operating in 1914 in Hamlet Hall and may have begun functioning up to three years earlier when Hamlet came into being. In 1915, the school was moved to the newly constructed Trinity Lutheran Church, which was paid $37.50 a month for rent. From 1919 to 1924, the school was moved to a new Hamlet Hall for which the monthly rental was $50. School board members at that time were Andrew Battleson, president, M. C. Noer, Edward Iverson, and P. K. Smith. The school enlarged its district by annexing the Hankey School to the south and the Willow Lake School to the north. The board selected Knut Vatne and M. I. Lysne to represent the newly annexed territory.

A variety of issues requiring action came before the school board. They included authorizing construction of school buses and hiring drivers, renting temporary quarters for the school and clarifying the rental terms, granting permission to students to take school-owned books home for study, authorizing teacher contracts, and issuing warrants to pay teachers' salaries. Because the district did not have enough money to write checks, they paid salaries by issuing warrants, which were certificates that could be sold at a discount to a bank or to others who wanted to buy them.

When the board rented Hamlet Hall on August 6, 1921, they did so "with the understanding that if dances and entertainments are given, the hall must be thoroughly washed and restored to a proper condition for school purposes before commencement of school hours." On November 5, 1921, the board voted to instruct the principal "to see that a sufficient amount of water is kept on hand at all times to meet the needs of the pupils." Water pails for drinking stood in a corner of the room, each pail with a dipper used by all. On November 17, 1923, they scaled back play time during recesses and the noon period to allow school to close at 3:00 p.m. "until the days are lengthened."

A list of 100 books in the school library during the 1918-1919 school year suggests what students may have been reading in addition to text books. One-third of the list included: *Robin Hood, A Child's Garden of Verses, Lowell Poems, Whittier Poems, Tennyson Poems, Alice in Wonderland, North Dakota Blue Book, The Golden Fleece, Black Beauty, Longfellow Poems, Carpenter's Geography Reader, King Arthur and his Court, Hans Andersen's Stories, The Tale of Peter Rabbit, The Tale of Benjamin Bunny, Best Stories to Tell Children, Baby Blue to his Friends, Mother Goose Village, Little Lord Fauntleroy, Dickens' Christmas Carol, Lessons on Manners, American Hero Stories, Norse Stories, The Overall Boys, The Story of Black Sambo, Puss in Boots, The Three Pigs, The Little Hen, Tom Thumb, Autobiography of Butterfly, Aesop's Fables, Stories of Country Life, Uncle Tom's Cabin* and the *Life of Abraham Lincoln.*

The most important action taken by the school board during this period concerned the construction of a new building for the school. At a July 5, 1919, meeting, the board voted to drive to Epping on July 12 to examine their new school building built three years earlier, in order to get ideas for the new structure planned for Hamlet. As plans developed, the board called a special election in the district to authorize issuing bonds in the amount of

The Hamlet School, built in 1923-24.

$30,000 at four percent interest to finance the construction of the school and to authorize increasing the district's debt by five percent. At the special election, thirty-eight votes were cast favoring the authorization and thirty-three voted against. Board members at the time were Andrew Battleson, Edward Iverson, Knut Vatne, Hans Olson, and William Smith.

During the years prior to the opening of the new school, the board discussed the condition of the school grounds, debated digging a well for the school and hiring the men to do it, hiring the first superintendent, purchasing desks and chairs, authorizing a full high school curriculum, setting the date for the school to open, and dedicating the building. They decided to pay Sander Olson 35 cents an hour to build a fence around the grounds and to plant trees. The fence was to be of "woven wire" with wooden posts four to five inches in diameter, with corner posts of steel. They voted to buy 100 trees from the Owatonna Nursery in Owatonna, Minnesota, for $95. They set the dedication for Thanksgiving Day 1923, and selected a committee of five women to arrange the dinner. The board also decided that "some speaker be arranged, if possible." They were able to get their first choice, Minnie Nelson, state superintendent of schools.

On March 22, 1924, the board hired W. C. Miles as their first superintendent at an annual salary of $5,000 and instructed him "to hire all the other teachers . . . with certificates of suitable standing and grade to entitle the school to state aid." They also authorized four years of high school instruction "if necessary" and set September 15, 1924, as the date for beginning the school year. Coal for the coming year was purchased at $2.50 per ton. With the completion of the new structure, Hamlet had facilities for twelve grades with four classrooms, a science room, a home economics room, a library, a superintendent's office, a gymnasium, restrooms, dressing rooms, and a boiler room large enough to house both the boiler and the coal needed to generate the steam that heated the building.

All communities in the area took pride in their schools. The buildings provided space not only for classes but for other community events as well. Sports teams, especially basketball, and musical groups were formed. Glee clubs and bands provided not only musical education for students but also offered the people living in the area a variety of entertainment. Life was not to be just about earning a living.

Striving to provide rural students services equal to those provided to town youth, the Hamlet board provided transportation to country students for the first dozen or so years after the new school opened in 1924. On my first day of school in September 1936, a neighbor who was paid to provide our transportation picked up children from three families in our area and drove them to school in his Model T Ford. Two boys sat in the front seat, and six girls squeezed into the back seat. I had with me a pencil that cost a penny, a tablet that cost a nickel, and a box of eight crayons that cost a dime—at the time considered adequate supplies for a beginning student.

During the winter, the driver used a team of horses pulling a bus on a sleigh. He arrived promptly at 7:45 a.m. at the Svendsbye farm and deposited the students at school shortly before 9:00 a.m. He spent the day in town, lodging the horses in the Hamlet livery barn, then visiting at the general store, the post office, and the elevator. He picked up the students at 3:30 or 4:00 p.m. and returned them to their homes an hour later. For the sake of safety, everyone stayed in the bus the entire time. But when the weather got nice in the spring, on the way home we occasionally yielded to the temptation to jump out the back door and ride on the rear runners of the sleigh. By the time we arrived home we were famished and devoured part of a loaf of bread our mother had baked while we were at school.

In 1938 or 1939 the busing stopped. Anders and a neighbor took turns driving their children to school for a couple of years, using a car when the roads were open. When the neighbors no longer had children in the Hamlet school, Anders became the sole driver. When working in the fields in the spring, he was often pressed for time, so the children walked approximately three miles to town, which took about an hour.

When I was in first grade, the school had four teachers using that number of classrooms, one each for grades one through three, four through six, seven and eight, and high school. With three elementary grades in one room, the class periods were fifteen minutes in length. Each teacher stayed in one room. By 1940 the number of teachers had dropped to two, with six classes in two rooms. The superintendent doubled as the janitor, which mainly meant keeping the heating system going, with some occasional sweeping of the floors.

During the 1941-1942 school year, the school board made an adjustment that may not always have been adopted by some schools. Hamlet's teachers that year were a married couple, Noel and Ferne Russell. Mrs. Russell became pregnant about the time the school year started. The

Russells brought the matter to the attention of the school board, chaired by Anders. Mrs. Russell's baby was due in mid-May, and the school year was not scheduled to complete its work until the end of that month, so the board simply changed the weekly schedule to include more hours per week in order to reach the state required minimum hours for all grades for the school year by the end of April. At that time the school closed to allow Mrs. Russell to have her baby on schedule without having to teach at the end of her pregnancy.

At that time, students in grades seven and eight were required to take state examinations to pass from one grade to the next. The school's record on that score was very good. When I reached grade eight in 1942 (I had completed grades six and seven in one year), the high school had closed the previous year, and Hamlet had become a one-room school like the ones it replaced twenty years earlier. By that time there were only twenty students in all eight grades.

However, even when using only a single classroom, the Hamlet school was better equipped than the usual one-room school. It had a reasonably large library that had been chosen for a school with twelve grades. Both the number and subject range of books was much greater than for a typical one-room school, a fact that was very important in the education of any student who used the library frequently. Hamlin Garland was my favorite author. I repeatedly read *Boy's Life on the Prairie* and *Son of the Middle Border*. With only one room in use, the entire school building was no longer heated. The running water was stopped. A coal-burning stove was put in the corner of the room, and a jug of water was provided for drinking. Two chemically-treated toilets were placed in the two lavatories, so it was not necessary for students to go outside to a toilet, as was done in earlier times. Electric lights remained, as did the indoor gymnasium, which though unheated could be used during recess and noon hours.

Some traditions came to an end in eighth grade, either because the teacher was male or for lack of time. In all prior years in elementary school, the teacher had begun each afternoon by reading a few pages from a book, like *Tom Sawyer* or *Uncle Tom's Cabin*. In that way, even students who did not read much got introduced to these classics, but that tradition went by the wayside. A less academic practice that also disappeared was the ritual observance of the teacher's birthday. It was somewhat like celebrating the birthday of the Queen of England; it didn't need to be done on the actual date. Once a year we chose a day and instructed all students to buy a small bag of unshelled peanuts, costing a few pennies. At the prescribed moment—presto!—we would open the bags and throw all the peanuts at the teacher, after which we sang "Happy Birthday." Each year the teacher acknowledged the honor—as the students scrambled to pick up the peanuts from the floor and eat them. Despite the school's shrinkage to eight grades, one teacher, and one classroom, other traditions or rituals continued. Each morning the flag was raised. Students continued to be taught the Pledge of Allegiance, although daily recitation was not practiced. We were taught to sing the "Star Spangled Banner," which was sung from time to time with gusto. Brief recess periods were regularly observed without supervision.

We each carried our own lunch and ate at our desks. For our family, lunch consisted of sandwiches. Few, if any, students brought fruit or vegetables. For a couple of years, an office representing Williams County distributed dried fruit, mainly apples and apricots. That fruit, together with raisins, was prepared as a fruit soup by a woman from the community who was paid a modest salary.

Snowstorms seemed to create their own histories. A mid-March storm in 1943 was so vicious it closed the school for four days. We siblings celebrated the vacation. East winds were so strong that snow filtered into our kitchen through the exterior door, requiring that the floor be swept and mopped almost hourly. Rags were stuffed between the door and the sill in a half-successful effort to keep the snow out. When we needed to go outside to water the animals or do other chores, our moves had to be planned carefully. We had to keep in sight of one another as we walked from the house to the barn and back so that we didn't get lost in the storm. After three days of pounding from the east, the wind switched to the northwest but snow continued to filter into the house. Snowdrifts higher than the barn, packed hard by the unrelenting wind, formed in the middle of the yard.[2]

During the storm, neighbors telephoned one another to see how things were going. One neighbor had gone to Tioga before the storm erupted and couldn't get back until the storm was over. On the first day of the storm, his wife told a neighbor that they had run out of hay and there was nothing to feed the cattle. After a day or two, they began bellowing loudly whenever anyone entered the barn. When the storm cleared, neighbors moved quickly to get hay to those cattle. Such cooperation was necessary and common.

Near the end of each school year the school sponsored a picnic for the students and their families. It was held just north of town, near a grove of trees that provided a more festive setting than the stark prairie. Blankets or tablecloths were spread on the grass, and on them the mothers placed salads, biscuits, watermelons, and lemonade for the crowd. Someone bought hot dogs and marshmallows for roasting over a carefully watched fire. The activity of the day was always softball.

With the Hamlet school reduced to eight grades in 1942, education through grade twelve was, for the first time in twenty years, no longer available in the home community. Anders' and Gudrun's daughter Gladys enrolled in the high school at Ray, boarding for the school week at a private home. Anders drove her to Ray every Sunday in the late afternoon and picked her up after school on Friday.

At the end of the 1942-1943 school year, Hamlet held its last graduation ceremony, this time for only five eighth graders. But the ceremony was as grand as ever. We marched in to a tune which I cannot recall, played by a local pianist. Pastor Harold Grindal from the Lutheran Free Church in Tioga spoke, and Jewell and Ardella Halgrimson, McGregor High School students, played a clarinet-saxophone duet. I delivered the valedictorian's address, and Willis Lokken the salutatorian's—both written by the teacher. Anders, as president of the school board, proudly awarded the diplomas. The school remained open for grades one through eight for another eighteen years, with one teacher who generally resided in the school. In 1960, with only nine students attending, the school closed, and the students matriculated at Wildrose.

In 2006, when the Wildrose-Alamo school also became a casualty of North Dakota's declining rural population, only four school systems were left operating in Williams County: Grenora, Ray, Tioga, and Williston. At one time, most towns in the county had had a school with twelve grades. During the decades of their existence, all served their communities well.

When North Dakota celebrated the 100th anniversary of its statehood in 1989, Chuck Suchy, its "centennial troubadour," recorded "One-Room School," in which he paid tribute to that educational icon. Strange as it may sound to persons educated in larger schools, I believe I received an excellent education in the kind of setting Suchy honored. Consider only this: Students could listen to the class or classes ahead of them and get started on more advanced class work, while at the same time listening to classes behind them and reviewing what they had learned in previous years. While in college or in a couple of the nation's best graduate schools, I never regretted having gone to a one-room school.

Churches

Another important institution that shaped life on the prairie was the church. Because the immigrants came chiefly from Scandinavian nations where the Lutheran Church was the state church, most of the early congregations in the area were Lutheran. While the vision of the immigrants for their church was guided by what they had known in Europe, it also incorporated a special American ingredient: religious liberty. The immigrants were happy to join this experiment because it gave them freedom and independence in the exercise of their faith.

The homesteaders were free to choose what church, if any, to belong to, and what confessional position they as members of a congregation should take. Church membership on the prairie was not automatic. It required two important decisions: First was the decision to join a particular congregation. Equally important was the decision, for Lutherans, which national Lutheran church body they wanted their local congregation to join.

Congregations were organized before the members had built a space to house them. Tioga organized its first congregation in 1903 in the sod house of John and Bertha Nesset whose two-part building was divided between a house and barn. Churches were organized in both McGregor and Wildrose in the year they formed the towns. Zion Lutheran of McGregor organized in the farm home of John Bergemoen, three miles south of the new town. The Wildrose Lutheran Church was formed by a merger of two predecessor churches, Immanuel and St. Paul, formed in 1904 and 1906 respectively. The two churches in Hamlet were organized about a decade before there was enough money to erect church buildings.

One prairie congregation was not large enough to be financially self-sufficient, so parishes were formed, each of which included three to five congregations in the area. Three parishes, one affiliated with the Norwegian Synod, one with the United Norwegian Lutheran Church, and one with the Lutheran Free Church, ultimately built parsonages in Wildrose. At first the pastors traveled to rural congregations with horse and buggy. As roads were constructed and automobiles came into use, the pastors crisscrossed the countryside by car so that worship could be held in each place at least once a month.

Stordahl Congregation

The Hamlet community, like its neighbors, organized congregations almost as soon as the immigrants had constructed their houses. The first was Stordahl, located four and one-half miles south and two miles west of the future Hamlet town site. It was organized on May 29, 1904, by Pastor Stener Svennungsen, although the group had worshiped together since the previous fall. According to O. M. Norlie in his *Norsk Lutherske Menigheter i Amerika*, Stordahl started with thirty-six souls, with one Swede, as members. The congregation was affiliated with the Norwegian Synod and by 1913 had constructed its church building on land donated by C. J. Helle. Money was scarce. In 1914 the congregation formed a parish with three other congregations and contributed $100 annually to the pastor's salary for that parish.

During the month that Stordahl was organized, Thor Birkelo and his two daughters arrived in the area. At some point, Thor, Gjertru, and their children joined the congregation. In 1914 Thor was a Stordahl trustee, which suggests that the family participated in the life of the congregation. Four of the Birkelo children took confirmation instruction at Stordahl, but were confirmed in the church in Wildrose. The two congregations were in the same parish. Sigurd was confirmed on July 20, 1913, when he was eighteen years old. Inga, Theodore, and Gudrun were all confirmed at the same time, on July 30, 1916. Inga was nineteen, Theodore sixteen, and Gudrun was fifteen, They were confirmed by Pastor Gustav Hegg, a graduate of Luther College in Decorah, Iowa, and Luther Seminary in St. Paul. He had been ordained in the Norwegian Synod in 1908 and became pastor in Wildrose in 1912, serving that and several other congregations for nine years.

Grong Lutheran Congregation

The congregation in Hamlet that became most important to the Svendsbye family was Grong Lutheran, of which Anders was a charter member. It was organized on July 20, 1905, by Pastor Bernhard Tollefson. Born in Ibestad in northern Norway, he attended Augsburg Seminary in Minneapolis and was on the clergy roster of the United Norwegian Lutheran Church in America. The congregation was also served briefly by Pastor Aslak Gunnarsen Lee of the Lutheran Free Church in Tioga. In 1906 the congregation divided into East Grong—in Hamlet—and West Grong. The latter soon took the name Ibestad. In 1914 it merged with another congregation to form Bethel Lutheran Church. East Grong immediately became simply Grong of Hamlet. It had a membership of forty in 1907 and forty-two in 1914. In 1905 the congregation paid its pastor an annual salary of $25, which had increased to $125 by 1914. In 1915 Elling Svendsbye was secretary of the congregation, and Anders was a deacon. The congregation had a denominational affiliation with the United Norwegian Lutheran Church in America. When Anders and Gudrun were married in 1918, Gudrun joined Anders as a member of Grong.

Grong was given its name by Elias and Margareta Strand, both born at Grong, Norway, about thirty miles east of Namsos, north of Trondheim. They had been married in Grong, immigrated to Granite Falls, Minnesota, in 1880, and in 1904 home-steaded in Section 21 of what became Big Meadow Township. They were among those who organized the Grong congregation in 1905, when Elias was elected a member of the first board of deacons and was its first treasurer. After its organization, Grong faced two important problems. Like other immigrant congregations on the prairie, they lacked an adequate place to worship and had no resident pastor. Ten years elapsed after its founding before Grong was able to

Grong Lutheran Church, Hamlet, North Dakota, a member of the United Norwegian Lutheran church in America, built in 1915, to which the Anders Svendsbye family belonged. Eight of the children were baptized here, and nine of them were confirmed here.

construct its building in 1915. The structure likely was built by labor from the community, perhaps including Ole Hove and Elling Svendsbye, both carpenters. In response to some members of the congregation, the building was constructed inexpensively and sparsely furnished.[3]

The interior walls were plain boards, stained brown. The altar was a simple table covered with a white cloth, embroidered at the ends. On it stood a small brown bowl which perhaps cost 10 cents, used as a baptismal font. On the wall behind it hung a small picture of Jesus at prayer, purchased by a Sunday school class. There was no kneeling rail in front of the altar, so members of the congregation stood when celebrating Holy Communion. A coal-burning stove, which members took turns getting started, was at the left front as one faced the altar. In front of the stove was a reed organ and in front of the altar was an upright piano. The pulpit stood in the right front. Behind it, in the corner and on a clothesline, hung a red cloth, behind which the pastor put on his black robe. In the late 1940s an altar with a kneeling rail and a wooden corner closet were added. The five simple pews on each side of the center aisle, made of plain boards, could each accommodate six persons, giving the church an ordinary seating capacity of sixty. Four windows on each side of the building brought in daylight. The few light bulbs that hung from the ceiling could easily be reached without a stepladder when they needed to be replaced. The church's small entrance hall was often used by the men as a place to gather, smoke, and visit.

The church also served as a social center for the community. Because the church had no basement, the back one-third of the sanctuary was outfitted as a kitchen, which included a two-plate electric burner and cabinets with counters lining the entire back wall. Later the electric plate was replaced with a small electric stove with an oven. Water needed for cooking and cleaning was brought from members' homes. On evenings when there was worship, the women of the congregation took turns making coffee for the social hour at the end of the service. The coffee usually started to brew near the end of the pastor's sermon, sending a welcome aroma throughout the sanctuary—and perhaps signaling the pastor not to preach overly long.

Through their Ladies Aid, the women of the church served an annual fund-raising dinner featuring lutefisk, meatballs, and lefse. People from neighboring communities came in large numbers to eat and visit. The Ladies Aid also held an annual auction at which they sold handwork, mostly items they had crocheted, knit, or embroidered.

Grong belonged to a five-point parish, which precluded weekly worship. Services were held once a month in the evening, because Grong was in a town that had electric power. The Svendsbye family regularly attended the monthly service when roads permitted. Anders and Gudrun also were able to worship at other times, courtesy of KLPM, the Minot radio station. It broadcast a Norwegian service on Sunday mornings, led by the Rev. Clarence J. Carlson, pastor of the Lutheran Free Church congregation in Minot.

The two Grong pastors who worked closest with the Svendsbye family while most of the children were growing up were Mathias Jacobson Berge and Olav Lin. Born at Stårheim, Nordfjord, just a few kilometers from where Gjertru Birkelo was born, Berge immigrated to the United States at age twenty-one. He had had limited schooling in Norway, so most of his education occurred as an adult in the United States, culminating in his graduation from the United Church Seminary in St. Paul. After serving a parish in Wisconsin, he came to Wildrose in 1912. He baptized Margaret Svendsbye on July 5, 1914, at a service in the Edward Iverson home and buried her mother, Lina, a year later. He performed the marriage ceremony for Anders and Gudrun, baptized five of their children, and confirmed one child.

Olav Lin, born near Kongsberg, Norway, immigrated to the United States at age sixteen. He attended Augustana Academy at Canton, South Dakota, and graduated from St. Olaf College in Northfield, Minnesota. Then he studied at the University of Oslo, before returning to the United States to teach for a few years, including one year at St. Olaf College as an instructor in Norwegian. After graduating from the United Church Seminary in 1914, he served two parishes in Minnesota before coming to Wildrose in 1929. He baptized four of the Svendsbye children and confirmed seven of them.

Pastor Mathias Jacobson Berge, pastor of Grong from 1912 to 1929 (left) and Pastor Olav Lin, pastor of Grong from 1929 to 1945 (right).

Pastors Berge and Lin both preached in Norwegian as well as in English. When Pastor Berge arrived in 1912, Norwegian was the sole language used, but in the 1920s English was introduced amidst controversy. By the time Pastor Lin came in 1929, English had become the primary language, with only occasional services in Norwegian.

Anders and Gudrun supported the use of English in the Grong church and wanted their children to speak English, but they felt compelled to show appreciation for the use of Norwegian as well. Only their oldest children understood Norwegian, but they brought the entire family to the Norwegian services, just as they did to the English services.

The controversy over which language should be primary in church split the two Svendsbye families belonging to Grong. A letter that Elling Svendsbye wrote in 1929 to his brother Ole in Norway gives insight into how the controversy progressed. He tells Ole not only about the involvement of himself and Anders, but also of Ludwig Hovde, a former neighbor of Ole's who had immigrated to the Hamlet area from the Snarum community in Norway where Ole lived. Elling wrote that he had gone with his wife, Johanna, to the Ladies Aid at the Hovdes' home.

At Hovde's Ladies Aid, there were many men present that day. Anders was also there. There were so many men because we are having a bitter Church fight. Most of the time, I am in a fighting spirit. I lead the fight for Norwegian. On my side are the Hovdes, John Hedlund and Hovde's father-in-law.

There have been many private discussions. Not many people spoke until after the pastor and his wife left. Then they were more free to express themselves. The conversation got tough.

Mrs. Hedlund spoke for Norwegian. She was not easy to stop. She spoke both English and Norwegian. She argued that people could learn both languages.[4]

Pastor Berge left the parish and Grong sometime in 1929. Whether the argument about the use of Norwegian had become so contentious as to ruin personal relationships, thereby contributing to Berge's decision to leave, is not known. But the arguments went deep and reflected differing views among the immigrants about how they could best adapt to life in the new land. Elling and Johanna spoke Norwegian in their home and required their children to learn the Norse language. They insisted that their children be confirmed in Norwegian. With that strong commitment to Norwegian, their oldest children did not learn to speak English until they enrolled in the public schools. Anders and Gudrun, on the other hand, chose to speak English in their home. That is, except when they did not want their children to understand what they were talking about, in which case they spoke Norwegian. Their oldest children learned Norse, but as a second rather than primary language.

Even though the language controversy erupted in the church, it was not really a religious controversy. While some families believed that the Christian faith could best be transmitted in their native tongue, the controversy was more social and political than religious. It was largely a question of culture and heritage. Some immigrants felt strongly that all of Norwegian culture, not just the Christian faith, should be transferred to the United States. As it was, the government used only English, as did the public schools, and it was the primary language of commerce. But when some people wanted to move English into the pulpit, a battle ensued because those people saw the church as the last bastion for defending and retaining Norwegian culture.

After Pastor Lin arrived, English became dominant. Pastor Lin was single, and he was a solemn man who neither smiled nor laughed. Of average weight and height, his solemnity was underscored by two small physical deformities. First, the top of his head was slightly misshapen and he was completely bald. He wore a wig made of straight, coarse, very black hair that came midway down his forehead. Second, his right hand had only three fingers—a thumb, an unusually large finger in the middle of his hand, and a little finger about half the size it should have been. He always dressed formally: suit, white shirt, and tie—never a turn-around collar or even a colored shirt. He seemed shy and had difficulty visiting with people. He was usually silent and did not mix well with people. When shown a newly arrived baby, his response was always the same: "A picture of health!"

The Sunday evening worship for the Svendsbye family began with a little tension in the home. Anders wanted to arrive an hour early. Albert did not, so he purposely delayed starting to get ready and then proceeded to do so with studied slowness, all of which irritated Anders, who paced around the living room in silence, constantly taking out his pocket watch to stop and look at it for a long time, as though he had trouble seeing it. With a loud sigh, he would put his watch back in his pocket, only to repeat the ritual minutes later amidst growing tension. When Albert was finally ready, everybody piled into the Model A and drove off to church at fifteen miles per hour. Despite the delays, the family arrived before anyone else, sometimes even before Pastor Lin, and of course, observed things with interest.

Everything was ritualized. The service was scheduled to begin at 8:00 p.m. Precisely at 7:30, Pastor Lin came out of the church where he had been sitting alone behind a curtained-off space in the corner behind the pulpit, and went to the outdoor privy. There were no facilities in the church for washing hands. Lin returned to the church without stopping to talk with any of the families gathering in their cars. With the pastor back, the people quickly moved into the church. The women went in to sit in the back pews on the left side of the church, while the men remained in the entrance hall to visit until about five minutes before worship was to begin, which was the time for them to enter and claim their place in the back pews on the right side. All, that is, except for the two leading families who sat together on the right side near the front of the church, as a witness to the rest of the congregation that the days of sexually segregated seating should be over. The church was silent except for loud whispering in Norwegian between Gjertru and her neighbor, all of which could be heard throughout the church.

All waited for the organist, who was invariably late. Since nothing could proceed without her, she, not the pastor, controlled when the worship would begin. If she did not arrive by ten minutes after worship was to begin, Pastor Lin would come out of his curtained corner and go before the congregation. Knowing there were two other people in the congregation who could play both the organ or piano, he would look straight ahead as if staring into space and ask almost rhetorically: "Is there anyone here who could play for us tonight?" Silence. In a short while, the two women with such abilities turned to look at each other in silence. After a nod or two at each other, one of them would proceed to the organ or piano to play a hymn for the prelude, usually "Sweet Hour of Prayer."

The liturgy was very brief and simple. It was a modified version of the order of Morning Worship in the Concordia hymnal. It was interesting both for what was included and omitted. The chief components were prayers, hymns, and the sermon. The prelude concluded, Pastor Lin would appear in his black robe from behind the red curtain in the corner and kneel in front of the altar for the opening prayer. "O Lord, our Maker, Redeemer, and Comforter," he intoned, "we are assembled in Thy presence to hear Thy holy word. . . ." In retrospect, two things are clear. First, the prayer was trinitarian while avoiding the more cryptic. "In the name of the Father, and of the Son, and of the Holy Spirit." It was a cozier prayer, identifying a three-fold work of God, one each attributed to the persons of the Trinity. Second, the prayer stated the purpose of worship: to hear God's word. In other words, the sermon was central.

Following the opening prayer and opening hymn, announced by the pastor because there were neither bulletins nor a hymn board, was a second prayer, a confession of sins, the heart of which was, "we are sinful and unclean." After the confession, there was no absolution. Following the confession of sins was one reading from the New Testament, usually from the Epistles. Next was the Apostles Creed, never one of the more complicated ones. After the creed, the congregation sang another hymn, following which came the sermon, about one-half hour in length. After the sermon, there may have been some special music. My sisters often sang solos, duets, or formed a trio. When I was in grade 2 or 3, Willis Lokken and I sometimes sang a duet, "Take Time to be Holy," which we had first sung in Trinity Lutheran Church. This was followed by another hymn, the offertory, and the closing prayer. The latter confirmed that the service had done what it was intended to do. "We thank Thee that Thou hast taught us what Thou wouldst have us believe and do." The offertory, generally referred to as "the collection," was almost always taken by members of the two leading families, using what appeared to be aluminum plates.

The announcements came after the closing prayer and were done with great solemnity. Pastor Lin would come before the congregation holding his fairly large green appointment book. He would page back and forth in his book and then, after much deliberation, say, "God willing, there will be services here again four weeks from tonight." On rare occasions, he would have a second announcement. After further paging back and forth in his appointment book, he would close it and ask the congregation, "Are there any other announcements?" He would then focus his gaze on two people, one of whom he expected to say something. After much looking around at fellow members of the congregation, one of the ladies would announce a meeting of the Ladies Aid. "Will there be a meeting of the Young People's Society?" Pastor Lin then inquired. There was usually no answer because no one knew. After another silence, the pastor would say, "These are the announcements," which was the functioning dismissal of the worshipers. Pastor Lin then retired to the curtained box behind the pulpit to remove his robe while the congregation scattered, the women to the back of the church to set out coffee and cookies, the men to the entrance hall to smoke and visit, and the children to wherever they wanted to go.

The men not only gathered to smoke and visit in the entrance hall; on occasion they transacted business of the congregation. In 1946, for example, the newly named Evangelical Lutheran Church (formerly the Norwegian Evangelical Lutheran Church) held a national fund-raising appeal called the United Mission Advance to raise several million dollars for the national work of the church. How Grong should participate in that appeal was often discussed in the entrance hall by the men after worship. It was decided that each family should be asked to make a contribution. The treasurer circulated his list of all contributors and the amounts given so that everyone interested could know who gave what. Some families adjusted their gift upward to more evenly match the giving of their neighbors.

But there was a problem. A widow living in an unpainted shack on the edge of town and who was thought to have less income than anyone in the congregation had given too large a gift in the eyes of the male leaders of the congregation. Translated, she had given as much money as many of the leaders of the congregation had given, and they were embarrassed. How to deal with the widow's generosity? Her only known income was from the cream she sold from her cows and the eggs she sold from her chickens. The question was raised: Should a delegation call on the widow and tell her that her gift was too large and she should take some money back? After considerable soul searching, the men decided not to make the visit. But their embarrassment was not forgotten.

While I recall attending worship regularly as a child and paid attention as best I could, I have no memory of anything said from the pulpit except for a reference Pastor Lin made one Sunday to the fact that he had read Adolph Hitler's *Mein Kampf*—in German. I recall nothing of what he said about the book but the fact that he had read it in German has stuck with me all my life. Pastor Lin was regarded as something of a scholar and was considered well-read. When he died, his brother came from South Dakota to organize a public auction of his possessions. Several people attending the auction were astonished at what then was considered to have been a huge library, with many books in Norwegian and German.

Sometimes when the roads were closed because of snowdrifts, Anders or Albert drove the family to Hamlet with a team of horses pulling a sleigh with a wagon box on it. Bells were attached to the horses' harnesses, making a beautiful sound as they trotted across the snow-covered prairie. Somehow, it is easier to remember the sleigh ride than the worship service.

Holy Communion was always celebrated around Christmas and Easter and perhaps once more during the year. Only in the late 1940s, after Arnold Blom became pastor, did the practice of monthly communion develop. Although Anders and Gudrun were always present at such services, they rarely received the sacrament, because they did not consider themselves "worthy." Historically, the notion of being worthy grew out of the concern in the Church of Norway and Lutheran churches in some other countries about adequate preparation for communion. Through the years that concern degenerated into the notion of worthiness. The idea was that one should and could lead a moral life that would make one worthy to receive the body and blood of the Lord. A few of the neighbors regularly participated in the sacrament, but the majority of the congregation did not. One could hear occasional rumblings among the men standing around after the service as to why family X considered themselves worthy. "Didn't everyone know what had once happened in that family?" Anders and Gudrun made an exception to their non-communing practice. In an era when confirmation and first communion were, in effect, a single event for most Lutherans, they accompanied each of their children to the communion table as he or she was confirmed.

Sunday school was held in the Grong sanctuary every Sunday of the public-school year—when the roads were open. A valiant attempt was made to teach students Martin Luther's Small Catechism in its entirety over the course of several years. Despite yeoman efforts by the Sunday school teachers, however, they really did not get much beyond the Ten Commandments. Anders and Gudrun wanted their children to carefully study their Sunday school and confirmation lessons, but they never discussed the lesson contents with them.

Confirmation classes were held once a week in Grong Church during the three summer months, for two successive years, when the confirmand was twelve to fourteen years old and in grades 7 and 8 in the public school. The hour required to walk to Hamlet provided an opportunity to memorize the lesson on the way to class. The pattern for each class never varied. The class opened with the singing of the same hymn: "O Bread of Life from Heaven." With only four students and the pastor, the sound was not much louder than a whisper. The pastor emphasized what he called recitation. That is, at each class session he asked each confirmand to recite from memory the part of the catechism and the Bible verse(s) assigned for the day. No effort was made to find out if the confirmands understood what was memorized. No explanation was provided about the meaning of words and concepts, including such difficult words and concepts as justification. Memorization was sufficient so long as the material remained in one's memory bank at least until it was needed in the oral examination—or catechization—prior to the confirmation rite.

At the service prior to confirmation (about one month earlier) a public examination, called catechization, was held in the church. All the catechists were seated in the front row of the church. At the appropriate time, the pastor asked them to come forward to the altar. He then proceeded to ask each of the catechists a series of questions about Martin Luther's Small Catechism. The answers had been memorized prior to the examination so that it really became a test of the ability of each catechist to memorize. There were no questions to try to determine whether the student understood what he/she was saying. No one ever failed the exam, although some, like the Svendsbye siblings, were better at memorization than others. After the service, parties were sometimes held in various homes to celebrate the event. Since catechization was a public event witnessed by the entire congregation, Gudrun and Anders were proud because all their children came through with flying colors. On such occasions, each Svendsbye child was heavily praised during the car ride home following the service.

From a child's perspective, the big event of the church year was Grong's Christmas program, which primarily featured Christmas carols. Some years there was a choir combining adults and children. Each Sunday school student was assigned something to recite. The program was intended as a happy celebration, and it was. But with its many rehearsals, it was also one of the congregation's most effective teaching tools. Christmas was celebrated at both the church and the public school. While the church focused most of its carols on the Christ child, the school children gustily sang both "Jolly Old Saint Nicholas" and "Joy to the World." It is remarkable how similar the programs were. At the conclusion of both programs, a small paper bag of candy and nuts, and sometimes an apple, was given to each child. Money to purchase those gifts for the school children came from the entire community. During December, the Hamlet store and post office received donations from their customers for that purpose. Church members donated money to buy the gifts for the church program.

Pastor Lin served the congregation faithfully for more than a decade and a half. He died just before Christmas in 1945. At the time there was a shortage of clergy in the Norwegian Lutheran Church in America, so the pastorate remained vacant—and Grong was closed most Sundays—for one and one-half years. Pastors from Ray, Williston, and Crosby came to Grong for special events such as Christmas and Easter. A Luther Seminary student, Leon Holm, worked in the parish during the summer of 1946.

Anders regularly served on church boards. He also served on the call committee to select a replacement for Pastor Lin. On the morning after the committee decided whom to call, Anders was asked, "Why did you call Arnold Blom rather than either of the other two men considered?"

"Oh," he replied, "Blom sounded more Norwegian than the others did."

When Pastor Arnold Blom, a graduate of St. Olaf College and Luther Seminary, arrived in 1947, he introduced the parish to a different Lutheran liturgy and the use of different vestments. Grong had used a shortened version of the morning liturgy of the Concordia Hymnal since they started using English in their worship. They preferred that because it was simple, and they were not required to say much during the service. They preferred to sit and listen rather than do something. "Church" was the preacher's time, not theirs, and they came to hear what he had to say. He was to preach the Word as the opening prayer indicated. Several members of Grong never joined in singing any of the hymns, Anders and Albert included. They did not even look in the hymnal. They just sat and listened. Even the prayers were all said by the pastor only, even the Lord's Prayer when it was used. In addition to the hymns, the congregation only confessed the Apostle's Creed. Not even an "Amen" was anticipated. The liturgy was essentially an ode to simplicity. Pastor Blom persuaded the congregation to use the Common Service, a liturgy derived from Martin Luther's modification of the Roman Catholic Mass, which, with slight variations, was used by most Lutheran churches in America. It was more complicated than the simple Concordia liturgy and it called for much greater participation in the service than was the custom of the congregation. But the congregation, under Blom's leadership, learned it.

Pastor Blom also persuaded the parish to allow him to use the black cassock, white surplice, and stoles reflecting the different colors of the church year. Until Blom arrived, the pastors had worn simple black robes without stoles. This change, symbolically at least, was more important than the changes in the liturgy—even with the introduction of the absolution—because it accentuated the differences between the clergy and laity. For people coming from the Lutheran tradition that Grong embraced, such differences were to be minimized. Fancy vestments—akin to what kings wore—were to be banned because they might imply a higher order for the clergy, and it reminded church members of Roman Catholicism. This had been anathema to parts of the church in Norway and would have been the occasion for furious differences of opinion resulting in some trauma. But now, in the middle of the twentieth century, quietly, reasonably, and without rancor, Pastor Blom was able to introduce changes that moved the parish closer to the center of American Lutheranism. The changes were made peaceably, without resulting turmoil in the parish, perhaps due to Pastor Blom's friendly, non-authoritarian manner. He elicited trust and confidence in his person and managed to lead the parish in significant change without suggesting that it involved serious modification in either theology or ecclesiology.

The Grong church building was last used on Sunday, June 3, 1967, when eighteen people gathered for worship. Three years later the building was carefully torn down. Former members of the Grong congregation now worship in Wildrose.

Trinity Lutheran Congregation

There is disagreement about who organized the Trinity Lutheran Congregation. According to its records, the congregation was organized on Pentecost Sunday, June 3, 1906, by Pastor A. G. Lee, who was serving the Lutheran Free Church in Tioga and living in Palermo. The Williams County history states the organizational meeting was held at the Syver Thorseth home, north of the Hamlet town site on land owned today by Milton Nygaard. According to Norlie's *Norsk Lutherske Menigheter i Amerika*, Pastor Christian Georg Jørgensen, a native of Vik, Norway, and a graduate of Augsburg Seminary, Minneapolis, organized the congregation in 1906. He was living in Marmon, a postal station in Athens Township, about ten miles south of Zahl and twenty miles north of Williston. In 1908, Christopher Knudsen Ytrehus came from Alexandria, Minnesota, to be Trinity's regular pastor, residing in Wildrose. A native of Bremanger, Sønfjord, Norway, he too was a graduate of Augsburg Seminary. He served for six years. At the time it was formed, Trinity had a membership of sixty, growing to 141 in 1915.

Trinity's services were initially held in parishioners' homes. But after Hamlet came into being, at least one Hamlet Hall was built and used for community activities. The Trinity and Grong congregations both used that

Trinity Lutheran Church in Hamlet, a member of the Lutheran Free church, as it is being built in 1915.

hall for worship, although exactly when and for how long is not clear. According to an article in the county history, the Trinity congregation met in homes and in "the school house" before their church was completed in 1915. A story in the first issue of the *Hamlet Times,* published on March 14, 1914, said Christopher Ytrehus, pastor of Trinity Lutheran Church, would conduct worship and preach in Hamlet Hall on April 5. The county history says Hamlet Hall was constructed in 1919. If that is so, there must have been an earlier building by that name.

Trinity's building was constructed at a cost of $3,500 in 1914-1915. At about the same time, the Grong church was built, and the two new churches stood less that one-fourth of a mile from each other. The Trinity building was the more handsome structure. It had a bell tower, and the bell could be heard for several miles on a still day. That church had a basement, which meant the congregation could serve dinners and host other events much more easily than was possible for Grong. Trinity continued to operate for fifty-one years. The last person to be baptized there was Marlyn Vatne, grandson of Anders and Gudrun, on July 25, 1948. In 1957, the congregation disbanded because of decreasing membership.

Despite some differences between the two congregations, they were not the reason for the establishment of two Lutheran churches in the small town of Hamlet. The reason was not theological; it was geographic. The people who lived north of Hamlet chose Trinity. Those who lived south of Hamlet chose Grong. While the churches are now gone, the geographical difference remains—the Trinity cemetery serves those living to the north of town; the Grong cemetery serves those living to the south.

The geographical differences produced amazingly deep emotions in the larger community. When Trinity closed ten years before Grong, no one living north of town ever transferred from Trinity to Grong. While several chose to go to Wildrose, some did not transfer anywhere.

The Anders Svendsbye family early on became associated with Trinity. Two of its staunch members were Knut and Caroline Vatne, who lived two miles north of Hamlet, where they had homesteaded in Section 2 of Hayland Township in Divide County. They had two sons, Gilmer and Arthur, who married the two oldest Svendsbye daughters, Margaret and Alice. At the time of their marriages, Margaret and Alice joined Trinity and, as a result, the Svendsbye family began attending Trinity on special occasions. As life worked its way out on the prairie, family bonds appear to have been stronger than the bonds of church affiliation and even geography.

Related Identities

The Svendsbye family thus participated in the life of all three different Lutheran synods in the area—Stordahl of the Norwegian Synod, Grong of the United Norwegian Lutheran Church, and Trinity of the Lutheran Free Church. That participation was harmonious, but not without awareness of some differences. For example, Anders was happy about the marriages of his daughters, but one day, while reminiscing, he scratched his head and said, "I don't understand why Margaret and Alice had to marry someone from the Free Church." And once when Gudrun was talking about her relationship to the Stordahl congregation, where she was confirmed, she was heard to observe that "my family belonged to the real Norwegian Lutheran Church."

Because of rather strong feelings on the part of both Anders and Gudrun concerning their Lutheran identity, most members of the first generation of Svendsbyes held fast to that identity. Only two of them married non-Lutherans, and only two left the Lutheran Church. The two who left seemed content with their new affiliations—Roman Catholic and Evangelical Covenant/Baptist. Those who remained were active Lutherans. The situation is true for the second generation as well. Of the seventeen grandchildren of Anders and Gudrun, only three married non-Lutherans and only two joined different churches (Episcopal and Roman Catholic). Whether it was loyalty or preference at work is not clear. Maybe it was just the accident of geography at work.

CHAPTER 5

Struggling to Make Ends Meet

The grant of 160 acres of free land as a homestead did not mean instant wealth. Converting the prairie into profitable production was arduous work, and it went slowly. It also cost money. As the years went by, what had seemed like a possibility for inevitable success sometimes turned into a struggle for survival. This was the case for the Birkelo family.

The prairie, especially 160 acres of it, had lured Thor and Gjertru—and probably Anne as well—to borrow money to pay immigration costs. Hope abounded. But after settling on the prairie, indebtedness and borrowing mushroomed. Hardship or poverty seemed to stalk the Birkelo family like a disease. Money was needed beyond what the farm produced to cover costs of operation and even survival. For the Birkelos, difficulties mounted and ultimately triumphed.

The Birkelos Face Foreclosure

For them, 160 acres was not enough. Given costs, the rate of return on semi-arid soil, and the price of wheat, many homesteaders in the state were caught in the same bind. In retrospect, it is clear that Thor and Gjertru needed more land, but it is not clear that they saw that as a basic problem or imperative, or even a possibility. In any event, they did not buy more. Oral tradition has it that they rented an additional quarter section for a few years, but there are no records indicating they did so.

Thor and Gjertru had been adding to their indebtedness from the day they arrived on American shores. They borrowed money to come to the United States, and they borrowed more money to stay. In an effort to consolidate their debt, they borrowed $4,506 on December 15, 1919—a $2,500 mortgage from the McGregor State Bank and $2,006 from a friend, Olaf W. Nelson of Tioga. The bank immediately sold the mortgage to the Kinyon Investment Company of Owatonna, Minnesota.

While we do not know what payments, if any, Thor made to his friend, we do know that he did not meet the interest payments to the company, let alone pay down the principal. On December 9, 1924, the investment company appointed attorney Horace Bagley of Towner, North Dakota, to foreclose on the mortgage. Three days later, Bagley notified Thor that he had thirty days to pay the principal and accrued interest and taxes. A neighbor, Dagmar Bekkedahl, signed for Thor, acknowledging that he had been notified by registered mail. A notice of the mortgage foreclosure sale was published in the *Williston Herald* on January 22 and 29 and February 5, 12, and 26, 1925.

The foreclosure and sale occurred on the farm on March 4, 1925, at 2:00 p.m. under the supervision of A. R. Marshall, the Williams County sheriff. He sold the land to the Kinyon Investment Company, holder of the mortgage, for the total amount owed: $3,733. The price included $2,500 for the mortgage principal, $1,180 for interest, and $53 for fees.

Forced to leave their homestead, they moved everything they owned—horses, cattle, chickens, clothes, cookware, furniture, and machinery—across the road about one mile east to a two-room shack on the Nels Lorentsen homestead, which their son Sigurd attempted to buy. The frame structure had thin siding on the outside walls, without plaster or wallboard in the interior. The two-by-fours, visible from the inside, had nails where Gjertru hung all sorts of things, including four beautiful china cups. The kitchen was furnished with a cook-stove, table, cupboard, cream separator, and a few wooden chairs—nothing of comfort. The second room had space only for two beds along the north and south walls with a tiny space between them. They were also used for seating. The family clothes were hung in this room as well. In a shed attached to the house, they stored coal and vegetables. In the summer, Sigurd often slept there. Otherwise, he used the second bed in the room where his parents slept. This is a snapshot of the nation's rural poverty in the 1930s.

In this setting they lived out their lives as paupers—sometimes as wards of the Williams County Welfare Board.[1] Gjertru died on January 8, 1939, and Thor nearly two years later to the day, January 9, 1941. They now lie in Grong Cemetery, about one mile east from where they first homesteaded on the prairie. Ironically, seven decades later in 2008, mineral rights under their land could be leased for $150 per acre, or the tidy sum of $24,000 for 160 acres.

Thor and Gjertru were two people for whom the promise of America was never realized. They had begun their married life in a small village in western Norway. In their struggle with poverty, they moved their large family at least four times to other villages in Norway, trying to find a place where they could earn a sufficient income. When those hopes did not materialize, they did what thousands of other Norwegians had done; they immigrated to the United States on borrowed funds to join other members of their family in the quest for greater economic security. The Birkelos' quest ended in a two-room shack that did not even belong to them, set on a dry, dusty section of North Dakota's treeless prairie that was headed into a decade of drought. In the end, there were no more hopes and dreams. Here the Birkelos lived for another decade and a half without the benefit of a single advantage modern America made available to more fortunate folk: a warm house with adequate living space, at least one comfortable chair, electricity, running water, a telephone, a radio, an automobile, or a newspaper. Had they been able to foresee what would transpire, they might have stayed in Norway. They even needed help from their son-in-law, Anders Svendsbye, to pay their burial costs. But for all their poverty they retained a certain dignity, and the community honored them to the end. At Thor's funeral, for example, the choir sang no fewer than three anthems.

When Gjertru died in the Wildrose Hospital, Nurse Anderson, the sole staff member of the hospital, telephoned the Svendsbye farm just after breakfast on a Sunday morning and told Gudrun that her mother had died earlier that morning. When the conversation was over, Gudrun immediately telephoned Margaret and asked, "Did you hear the call?"

Margaret answered, "Yes." Gudrun then hung up the phone and burst into tears.

Told what had happened, Anders drove to the Birkelo farm to inform Thor and Sigurd, son of the deceased. After talking with them, he proceeded to McGregor to call on S. E. Spangrud, the community mortician. Spangrud drove his hearse to Wildrose to get the body and returned it to McGregor to prepare it for burial. When Anders returned home, he told Albert to harness a team of horses because they had to haul a load of wheat to the Hamlet elevator. In his conversation with Thor and Sigurd, Anders had been told that the Birkelos were completely broke and did not have any money to pay for the funeral. Anders had no choice but to pay the bill. He and Albert drove their team to the only granary on the farm that had some wheat in storage. Together they shoveled about fifty bushels into the grain box and set off across the snow-covered fields for Hamlet to sell the wheat. Wheat in 1939 sold for 62 cents per bushel, which meant Anders would get $31 to pay toward Gjertru's funeral expenses. If it were to cost more than that, it would have to be paid later. Afterward, a grave needed to be dug. Albert, Anders, Sigurd, and two neighbors brought picks, crowbars, and shovels to the cemetery to pry loose the frozen earth.

Almost immediately, the community swung into action. Day after day they brought all kinds of food to the Svendsbye residence—hot dishes, salads, biscuits, pies, cakes, and cookies. Gudrun, in turn, shared the food with Thor and Sigurd. That food took care of family needs for several days. It was the way the community chose to show their love and concern for their neighbors in time of sorrow.

The next step was for Pastor Lin to call on the family. Nobody heard his car arrive in the farmyard, and Lin did not get out of his car. Later in the afternoon, when Albert heard the dog bark, he opened the kitchen door to look outside to see what was disturbing the dog. Albert immediately went outside in his shirt sleeves to invite Pastor Lin into the house, past the growling dog. The family learned that Lin had arrived on the farm an hour earlier but had been too afraid of the menacing dog to venture out of the car to knock on the kitchen door. When safely inside, the only people who spoke during the visit were Pastor Lin, Gudrun, and Albert. Anders was absent. After being served coffee, Pastor Lin left.

Funerals were the most elaborate of the rites of passage in the Hamlet community. On the day of the funeral, the family waited in the car until the exact time for starting the service at Grong. After moving into the entrance hall of the church, they waited while the pall bearers went to the hearse to get the casket and carry it into the hall. Then Pastor Lin, robed in black, led the pall bearers carrying the casket from the hall into the church followed by the family, with Gudrun, Thor, and Sigurd leading the rest of the family, who took their places with the oldest first and the youngest last.

The hymnal used at Grong did not have a funeral liturgy, so the simple liturgy used on Sundays was followed. Interspersed among the prayers and sermon, the congregation and the choir each sang two hymns and Alice Vatne sang a solo. When the service was over, Mr. Spangrud, the undertaker, and his assistant wheeled the casket to the back of the church and opened it so that the congregation could view Gjertru as they filed out of the church. The family remained seated. When the congregation had exited the church, Spangrud and his colleague wheeled the casket back to the front of the church where the family was invited to view the body. Pastor Lin stood to the side, motionless and silent. I cried and started to walk away, but Gudrun saw me, came over, took my hand, and said, "Come and say goodbye to Grandma," as she led me back to the casket.

After about five minutes, Spangrud and his assistant came forward, covered the body, closed the casket, and wheeled it once again to the back of the church. At that point, the pall bearers, who had been waiting in the entrance hall, re-entered the church. The rest of the congregation, all of whom were dressed warmly, waited outside on the church grounds. Led by the pastor, the pall bearers carried the casket out of the church to the hearse, with the family following. Everybody got into their cars. Pastor Lin in his Model A Coupe, followed by the hearse and the family, led the procession as they and the congregation slowly drove the five miles to the cemetery. The cemetery gate was wide enough for the hearse to drive through to the grave site where the pall bearers carried the casket to the grave. The ceremony there was brief: ashes to ashes, dust to dust. After the neighbors had greeted the family, they, Pastor Lin, and a few neighbors drove to the Svendsbye farm where a meal was served by members of the congregation. Meanwhile, the casket was left in place over the open grave until everyone had left the cemetery. Then Spangrud and the pall bearers lowered the casket into the grave and filled it with dirt, closing the day.

Death had come earlier to the Birkelo family. Anne, too, died a pauper, or, as the court papers said, "Insolvent."[2] She died in 1908, but her estate was not settled for seven years. The final papers filed in the Williams County Court on September 8, 1915, by her brother, Kristen Birkelo, show that her debts exceeded the value of her estate.

Documents on file with the Williston Land Office tell a story about conflict between Kristen and Thor concerning Anne's estate. It appears that both, early on, were trying somehow to get title to or control of her land. On March 5, 1910, Thor, as an heir of Anne, filed his intention with the Williston Land Office that he planned to make Final Proof on April 10, 1910, "to establish claim to the land" involved in Anne's estate. Ten days later, Kristen wrote the same Land Office that "I make this affidavit for the purpose of denying that he [Thor] has done any work on this land since the death of my sister, the original claimant, and if he states in his proof that he has kept up the cultivation since the death of my sister he will be perjuring himself."[3]

Kristen contended that he himself had taken care of the land since his sister's death by employing a neighbor, Carl Sveen, to break ten acres in 1909, for which he paid Sveen five dollars per acre. Other documents show that the ten acres were sown with wheat in 1910.

While the brothers were filing counterclaims with the Land Office, the U.S. Census, dated April 15, 1910, records that Kristen was living with Thor and Gjertru Birkelo on their homestead. The two brothers must have discussed the matter, and Kristen must have persuaded Thor to relinquish his hopes, because he and his witnesses failed to appear in the Williston Land Office as scheduled, thus forfeiting his claim to the land. Kristen filed his own Proof for the land on May 17, 1910. Three weeks later, he was named executor of Anne's estate.

But Kristen did not let matters lie. He continued to vent negative feelings about Thor to the Land Office. The biggest problem he faced as executor was that no land on Anne's estate had been broken until after she died, even though the Homestead Act required that a few acres be cultivated. In a letter to the General Land Office in Washington, D.C., dated February 18, 1911, Kristen postured more than a little in describing all he had done to fulfill Anne's will. He reiterated that he had tried to persuade his brother to break some land for Anne, both in 1907 and 1908, but that Thor had said he had no time. Thor refused him, Kristen wrote, even though he "had furnished said person with four horses, wagon, and breaking plow, besides I have brought him over here on my own expenses, man, wife, and seven children."[4] That was true, but not exactly germane to the issues at hand.

Other documents show that on May 24, 1910, G. W. Wilson, register for the U.S. Land Office in Williston, issued a certificate saying that the heirs of Anne S. Birkelo had "made payment in full" for the SW ¼ of Section 11, on which Anne homesteaded, and "shall be entitled to a patent" on the land.[5] A year later, on May 18, 1911, the U.S. General Land Office in Washington, D.C. issued the patent to "the heirs and assigns . . . forever."[6] But on September 23 of that year, Kristen petitioned the Williams County Court for an "order" to sell the land. Judge A. L. Butler of that court granted the request on November 16, authorizing Kristen to sell. There are no other documents available on this subject until March 1915, when Anne's land became the property of A. R. Flugekvam.

In a Final Accounting dated September 8, 1915, Kristen, as executor of Anne's estate, reported that $129.72 was on hand as of September 22, 1911. To that was added $13 and $12 for the sale of hay on her land in 1912 and $93.75 in 1910 for the sale of wheat raised on ten acres of her land. He reported that he had paid bills amounting to $11.50 to provide a cement curb for Anne's grave, $1.50 for setting the grave stone, $9.15 for the tombstone, and $6.60 for the lettering. He paid $23.58 for real estate taxes in 1912, $16.41 in 1913, $21.10 in 1914, and $23.13 in 1915. The largest claim presented to the estate came from Anne's brother-in-law, Ragnald A. Flugekvam, who petitioned the court for $459.50, but was paid only $289.50 because of insufficient funds.

Kristen's final report as executor concludes:

> I pray that the administration of said estate may be brought to a close and that I may be discharged from my trust as executor. That after due notice given and proceedings had, the estate remaining in the hands of your petitioner as aforesaid may be distributed to the said part entitled thereto as aforesaid, to-wit: nothing to distribute.[7]

Anne's hope for new wealth in the United States ended with, in the words of the court record, "nothing." She is buried in the oldest section of Riverview Cemetery in Williston, marked by the little tombstone that cost her estate $15.75.

Here a strange twist must be noted. Exactly 100 years after Anne's death, rights to the mineral acres under her land could be leased for $150.00 per acre, or the sum of $24,000.00, as was the case for her parents' land. An oil company began drilling for oil in 2009.

Records in the Williams County Courthouse show that on March 18, 1915, Kristen Birkelo deeded his share of the land to A. R. Flugekvam, or Almer Flugekvam, son of Kristi Birkelo and Ragnald Flugekvam. Thor and Gjertru did the same with their interest in the land on March 24, 1915. On the same day, Ragnald and Kristi Flugekvam completed the transfer of their interest to their son. A. R. Flugekvam now owned Anne's homestead.

Tombstone for Anne Birkelo, 1908.

Anders Begins the Accumulation of Debt

Anders Svendsbye encountered financial challenges from the start, although in his first two decades in North Dakota things went quite well for him. According to documents filed with the U.S. Land Office in Williston, he began to break his land in 1906. In the spring of that year, Anders and Halvor Haakenson shipped an "immigrant car" on the Great Northern from Leeds, North Dakota, to Tioga. An immigrant car was a railroad car made available to immigrants at a very low rate to facilitate movement of animals, machinery, and household goods to the closest town where the immigrant lived. In it was a team of horses—Frank and Fanny—and a wagon owned by Anders. In a document the U.S. Land Office titled "Homestead Entry, Final Proof," filed in the spring of 1910, Anders testified that he built his house in 1905 and broke the first ten acres on his land a year later. There is no evidence that any of the ten acres was seeded that year. According to the same document, Anders broke an additional thirteen acres in 1907 and that year harvested ten acres of flax. In 1908, he broke seven acres and then fifteen acres in 1909, for a total of forty-five acres under cultivation. In 1908, he seeded twenty-three acres in oats and flax, and in 1909 thirty acres of wheat and oats.

That 1910 document suggests how quickly—or slowly—the prairie could be turned into tillable acreage, but does not report how much income Anders derived from his land each year. However, one can speculate with reasonable accuracy. The price of wheat in North Dakota in 1910 alternated during the year between 84 to 99 cents per bushel, averaging 91 cents. In 1909, the price average was 90 cents. The average per-acre wheat yield in 1910 was twenty-five bushels per acre and in 1909 just over twenty-four.

Assuming that twenty of the thirty acres Anders planted in 1909 were sown to wheat and that he had a return of twenty-five bushels to the acre, he would have harvested 500 bushels of wheat. At 90 cents per bushel, Anders' gross income in 1909 would have been $450—an amount that at the time must have seemed tremendous. (The oats likely were not sold.) It was seven times the amount of money he had when he arrived from Norway five years earlier, and he made that from a single growing season. He may well have thought he was on his way to realizing his dream of economic betterment in the United States. If he did, he was wrong.

Anders remembered 1915 as being one of his best years in farming. He talked especially about the return on his flax field. That summer, after Lina died, he and his friend Knute Berg took the train to St. Paul to see the movie *Birth of a Nation*—at a per-ticket price of $5. The cost of the trip and the movie suggest Anders' high interest in public affairs and his strong desire to know more about the formation of his adopted country.

There is no evidence to suggest that the racial bias of the film informed his thinking on the subject.

Despite what seemed a good financial return for those early years, Anders needed more money than the farm produced. He faced the same problem the Birkelos faced. He needed more than his cherished 160 acres could produce to make a go of it. To expand and develop his operations beyond his homestead, he needed more horses, more cattle, and more land. To finance all that, he would have to borrow money.

It appears from the records that Anders was in debt most of his life after receiving title to his homestead. He left dozens of records about his purchases of land, machinery, and animals. They may not be complete, but they offer insight into life on the prairie, the costs involved in starting and expanding a farm, and the struggle to survive during the drought and Depression. Much of the information is recorded on mortgages and notes issued by banks when Anders borrowed money to purchase machinery and land. The dated documents include the amount borrowed, the rate of interest, and an itemized list of whatever was given as chattel. Horses, cattle, and machinery were the principal items listed. The horses were listed by name, color, weight, and age; the cattle by color, weight, and age; the machinery by type, brand, and year of manufacture. Even chickens were used as chattel, with no description beyond their total number.

The use of credit was not unique to Anders or other immigrant farmers. It was part of the American way of life for both rural and urban people, as historian David Danbom illustrates in his history of the Fargo, North Dakota, community during the Depression. He found, for example, that in Fargo and adjoining Moorhead, Minnesota, in 1928, "Ninety percent of grocery purchases and sixty to seventy-five percent of department store purchases were made on credit." The rhythm of borrow and pay kept the national economy going and was representative of millions of people in the United States. The problem for Anders and thousands like him was that, during the 1920s and 1930s, the borrow-pay rhythm was interrupted when, at pay-up time, there was no money.

Anders was neither lazy nor a spendthrift. But the reality of "it's pay-up time, but there's no money" hit him hard during those two decades. Two calamities struck, about which he could do nothing; the national economy went into a Depression and the rainfall nearly stopped. Those twin disasters forced him and thousands of others to borrow money just to exist.

Economic hardship hit the farmers of the Midwest long before the stock market crash in 1929, pushing the need for existence borrowing back to the mid-1920s. Thus beginning in the mid-1920s and continuing through the drought and Depression of the 1930s, Anders was caught in a situation shared by many, if not most, of his neighbors: he could not even pay his taxes.[8] For several years he had to borrow money to pay for both the seed he planted each spring and for hay to feed the animals. As years passed without enough income to pay either interest or principal on his debts, some creditors wrote harsh letters in attempts to collect.

These were cruel and troublesome times for everybody—borrowers and lenders alike. Each farming season began with renewed hope that this year would see enough rainfall to produce a good crop and that the market would pay an adequate price for the harvested grain so that bills could be paid and debts honored. But year after year the rains did not come in adequate amounts. Instead, strong winds blew across the dry fields. The dust rose and was airborne for hundreds of miles as the cultivated land lost several inches of necessary and valuable topsoil. There were times when there was enough rain to get some kind of a crop, but then the grasshoppers came. They could destroy fields in a hurry. At other times hail and rust damaged crops in varying degrees.

The story of Anders' financial difficulties began when he bought his first machinery on credit. Later he borrowed money to buy land to expand his farm modestly beyond his homestead. But when the two calamities of nature and the economy came with vengeance, he was forced to borrow money to keep his family and animals alive. Without adequate income as time unfolded, he became a regular customer of banks and other lending institutions.

At the time of his first harvest in 1907, he owned no harvest equipment. He had to borrow a binder from a neighbor or, more likely, had to cut the grain the old-fashioned way, with a scythe. He was accustomed to using a scythe from his farming days in Norway. Also, he likely did not own a drill for the first year or two, in which case he may have sown his grain crops by hand, as he had done in Norway. By the following year, however, Anders was in business and in debt. By now he had purchased three more horses and a binder for cutting grain. On August 8, 1908, he purchased a seven-foot Deering binder for $60 from Nels Simon, co-owner of the International Harvester dealership in Tioga. To secure the $60 note, he mortgaged Fanny, his eleven-year-old, 1,300-pound bay mare, valued at $140. The note carried a charge of eight percent interest and was due October 1, 1909. If not paid until after maturity, the note would have drawn interest at ten percent. Anders paid off the note on September 25, 1909, just in time to avoid the penalty.

In January 1909 he mortgaged his five horses to borrow $250 from the Linwell State Bank in Ray. (Hamlet, Wildrose, and McGregor did not yet exist. Later, Anders did his business there.) Given the value of horses at that time (Fanny had been valued at $140.00 a year earlier, and Thor Birkelo bought a team of horses in 1905 for $275.00), it seems excessive for the bank to have required that all five horses be given as chattel for a $250 loan. The horses were listed by name and age: Frank, twelve years; Fanny, twelve; Daisy, twelve; Maud (the name of Norway's new queen), seven; and Cauky, nine. On April 23 of the following year, Anders borrowed another $650 from the same bank and mortgaged a quarter section of land.

The inadequacy of a 160-acre farm was soon pressing with greater force. But to remedy the situation would require more borrowing and mortgaging. In this respect, Anders was typical of other farmers struggling to make ends meet. According to Robinson, "half of farms operated by their owners were mortgaged in 1910, seventy-one percent in 1920." On March 12, 1913, Anders and Lina doubled the size of their farm. They bought an adjoining quarter section of land from Ingeborg Anderson Roll and Bernhard Roll for $3,200. They paid $900 in cash, assumed the $700 mortgage on the land, and borrowed an additional $1,600. The amount borrowed was repaid in four equal installments, plus eight percent interest, in each of the years 1913 through 1916. They moved to the newly acquired quarter section because it had a larger house. A barn, chicken house, granaries, and a garage were constructed on the property later.

Anders A. Svendsbye in 1915.

Then, in 1915, Lina died. For a couple of years following her death, Anders appears to have been uncertain about the future. He quit his regular farming operations for a year while his brother Elling used his horses and machinery. Anders apparently had oxen and used them during this interlude to break additional acreage. The scant evidence that is available suggests that he was somewhat mystified as to how life as a single parent would unfold on the prairie. He needed time to think as he crisscrossed his land behind the slow-moving oxen, turning over furrow after furrow of the grassland. Whatever his thoughts, he seems to have kept them to himself and stoically mourned in private.

In 1917 Anders bought an impressive quantity of trees to be planted—500 green ash, 1000 laurel willows, and 500 poplars—for $70 from the Northwest Nursery Company of Valley City, North Dakota, giving him the largest tree field in the immediate area. However, the trees did not provide much of a windbreak, because the barn was located where the trees should have been planted. Instead, most of the trees had to be planted south of the house, where, as they grew, they partially blocked the view of the highway. Many farmers did not like to do that, because they preferred to see who was driving by and who was driving from the highway into the farmyard. In any event, the tree field south and west of the house soon gave a new dimension to prairie life. But even after the trees had attained some fullness, it was hills, not the trees, that blocked the Svendsbyes' view of the prairie, especially to the south and west.

A New Life But Still Debt

By 1918, Anders was ready to begin a new life. A seventeen-year-old neighbor girl, Gudrun Birkelo, had caught his eye. She lived one mile north of his farm and had helped her mother, Gjertru, care for Anders' daughter, Margaret, after Lina had died. This was Anders' second romance on the prairie, and few details survive about either. There were silent movies in Wildrose, as well as bars and dances in neighboring towns, but neither Anders nor Gudrun had an interest in such activities. Anders taught Gudrun how to drive his new Dort automobile. However the attraction developed and grew, Anders and Gudrun were married in the Lutheran parsonage of Pastor Mathias Jacobson Berge in Wildrose on December 5.

Their marriage unfolded into a faithful, hardworking companionship. It marked a new beginning and a new determination to make things move forward. It seems to have paved the way for a new phase of farm expansion and borrowing. The first of the major financial arrangements had preceded the wedding, occurring on February 8, 1918, when Anders borrowed $2,000 from the Federal Land Bank in St. Paul at five percent interest and mortgaged Roll—the quarter section he bought in

1913. On January 8, 1919, Anders and his new bride borrowed another $2,000 from the Federal Land Bank at five and a half percent interest and mortgaged Anders' homestead. Finally, on November 22, 1919, the couple borrowed $2,000 at six percent interest from the First State Bank of Hamlet and mortgaged the Kinneberg quarter section, which they acquired with the loan.

The Hamlet bank note was due November 22, 1924. To pay it, Anders twice borrowed money from the same bank and listed his horses and cattle as collateral. He obtained $1,400 on September 27, 1923, and $1,300 on November 3, 1924. In 1923, his collateral included nine horses and thirty cattle, of which ten were milk cows. In 1924, he had eleven horses and thirty-eight cattle. The horses were again listed by name, color, age, and weight. The nine horses named in 1923 were Rowdy, Barney, Cora, Little Queen, Dan, Prince, Big Queen, Maud, and King. A year later he added Rex and Ned and replaced Maud with Topsy. During the 1920s, Anders owned eleven horses, enough to use two rigs simultaneously in separate operations. That required employing a hired hand during the growing, haying, and harvesting seasons, who often was Gudrun's youngest brother, Theodore.

At first, Anders was able to meet his principal and interest payments on time. But by the mid-1920s, he began to fall behind the payment deadlines, and his loans became delinquent. His situation was shared by many of his fellow farmers in the state. As Robinson recounted, "Most of the farm-mortgage loans became delinquent (78 percent of Federal Land Bank loans in 1933), and the number of forced sales increased."[9] Anders' delinquency led to a threat from the Federal Land Bank on September 30, 1931, to foreclose on the loans. In time, for reasons that are not clear, the bank decided not to foreclose but to continue the loans, even though delinquent. Anders was deeply grateful. He wanted desperately not to lose his land and was willing to pay the price of a growing accumulation of interest.

The decision not to foreclose distinguished Anders' financial situation from that of his father-in-law. In Thor's case, the banks foreclosed, and the family was forced to move off what had been their land. Anders, on the other hand, was able to forestall foreclosure. He retained his land and lived on it until just a few years before he died.

Anders' borrowing continued throughout the decades of the 1920s and into the 1930s. In 1925, he borrowed $1,700; in 1927, another $2,000. For the larger amount, he had to mortgage machinery as well as nine horses and forty head of cattle. The machinery listed included a five-foot 1923 Deering mower, a ten-foot 1923 Deering hay rake, a ten-foot 1927 Van Brunt drill, and an eight-foot disk.

Debt Collectors and Debt Payments

Because of Anders' inability to pay the annual interest, much less payments on the principal, it is not surprising that implement companies, banks, and even local businesses began to press him for money he owed. Letters from collectors contained both inducements and threats. For example, on July 30, 1927, Anders and a neighbor had purchased a Nichols Shepard threshing machine at a cost of $1,378 for which, five years later, they still owed $220.84. Payment on the installments started out well but did not proceed as planned. One attorney attempting to collect from Anders wrote, in part,

> I am firmly convinced that there is only one way to collect the account, and that is to sue. However, if you and Mr. _____ together can obtain the sum of $20.84 to submit to me to apply on the account, I shall allow you an extension of time for settlement of the balance.
>
> I feel that this is a very fair proposition. For no remittance whatever has been made to apply to your claim in a period of over two years.
>
> You realize, I am sure, that the bank is entitled to the money, it is the bank's money, and you have withheld it for a very long time.
>
> I do not care to demand payment, but if you will not submit it amicably, I shall enforce the issue. Personally, I believe that if you are at all sincere in your alleged desire to do what is right and fair, you will exert a very strenuous effort to submit the amount requested.
>
> It is very small in proportion to the amount you owe, and I feel that between the two of you it should be simple to obtain. . . .[10]

The letter suggests intense frustration on both sides. The lender had extended credit in good faith and needed the money. He was likely nearly beside himself at all his failed efforts to obtain some payment from Anders and probably scores of others. On the other hand, Anders was almost without funds. As a man who wanted to pay his debts—and ultimately did—he must have felt an enormous burden and a different kind of frustration when such letters arrived and he had no money to submit as payment.

When creditors tried to collect even small amounts of what was due, their efforts were in vain. Anders had undertaken some purchases, like the threshing machine, in a more affluent moment and had never imagined a time would come when the crops would be so meager that he could not meet his payments. But by 1932, the rain had nearly stopped. He found himself unable to make even the smallest payments or to take advantage of the most reasonable settlement offers he received. Perhaps the harshest collection letter came from an agency working to collect final payments for a DeLaval cream separator the Svendsbyes had purchased from a hardware store in Wildrose:

October 30, 1930

Anders A. Svendsbye
Hamlet, North Dakota

B.C.S. Corp. Claim #277116
Unpaid Balance: $47.00
P A S T D U E: $23.50

Dear Sir:

You have a debt to pay!

We have written you courteously and considerately in regard to the money you owe our client, the B.C.S. Corporation.

Up to now, we have not been convinced that you were trying to avoid paying an honest debt. Further delay on your part, however, will convince us that you did not enter into this contract in good faith.

We can see no reason for being patient with a man who ignores his honest obligations.

You know you owe this debt and silence or pleading ignorance is not an excuse in the eyes of the law.

There is no excuse for this flagrant breach of contract. The case against you is too clear to waste any more time.

We shall expect full payment by return mail.

Yours truly,[11]

During the following year Anders made two payments of $23.50 each, which paid off that debt. Each payment was acknowledged with a curt, one-sentence letter, without a thank you.

Although debts were piling upon debts, Anders did, in fact, manage to pay small amounts on some debts in addition to the cream separator. On August 4, 1932, for example, he paid $12.40 to the Williams County Sheriff toward his delinquent personal property tax for 1924. But such payments were rare and never sufficient. There simply was no money available, even though that reality seemed hard for collectors to understand or admit.

Another example of a collection letter, one of the earliest Anders received, came from his friends and neighbors in McGregor, the owners of the Simon-Berg store. The Berg of that company was Knute Berg, Anders' closest friend, who came from the same community in Norway as Anders. Knute had recently died, but those who sent the letter were his friends and associates. There were very few of the firm's customers who did not receive a personalized version of this form letter:

8/30/21

Mr. A. Swnsby
McGregor, N. Dak.

Dear Sir:

Owing to the financial condition last fall, we were compelled to go through the season practically without money, because a majority of farmers refused to sell their grain and held on to it, thereby, sustaining big losses, and thus were unable to pay us, on account of lower prices.

This fall things will be different. We owe the wholesale houses large sums of money and they have already served notice on us that they MUST have their money this fall without fail. So you can readily see that there is nothing for us to do but to ask you to promptly pay your notes and accounts this fall.

We believe that the average man likes to pay promptly and more so, for groceries and machine extras that he uses for living and farming operations, but for some reason the first money goes to the banker and outside parties, and the home merchant is compelled to wait. This is not RIGHT. Your store and machine account should be paid first. Now, let us change this system and try to pay your home merchant first this year.

Your account with us $20.50

Notes amounting to $470.00

Note will be due and payable. 9-1-21

       Yours truly.

Simon-Berg Co.[12]

The letter illustrates how interdependent small communities were and how everybody suffered. Simon-Berg was over the barrel. They could not normally demand cash if they wanted to stay in business, because their regular customers seldom had much cash. Thus they were forced to extend credit. But when their customers could not pay them at the end of harvest, they in turn could not pay their bills, and the businesses to which they owed money naturally demanded payment. This is why thousands of pioneer farmers in Anders' position gave up, left their homes and property to the debt collectors, and moved to the West Coast or other places to begin life over again.

Anders and Gudrun decided to remain on their farm, and accomplished that through sheer force of will. As a matter of fact, despite the pressures they must have felt, they moved through the years with grace—calmly, stoically, hopefully, even thankfully—joining other neighbors and families across the nation in the annual celebration of Thanksgiving. To keep going, they received "relief" from the Williams County Welfare Board. To receive that relief dashed some of the hopes and expectations with which Anders had crossed the Atlantic three decades earlier, but accepting relief was an experience they shared with slightly more than half the population in North Dakota by late 1936.[13] In addition to the relief, they had to obtain dozens—maybe even hundreds—of small loans to survive. And, eventually, government at all levels—federal, state, and county—acted to help.

Anders retained a copy of a fascinating 1935 letter from the Federal Emergency Relief Administration for North Dakota and the state's Public Welfare Board that was distributed to relief recipients by the Williams County Welfare Board. The two agencies, one state and one federal, urged Anders not to pay his debts unless he was sure he had enough money to get through the months immediately ahead. They went so far as to tell him that if he used farm income to pay his debts, he would disqualify himself from receiving relief:

For Williams County North Dakota
Mr. Andrew Svendsby
Hamlet, N. D.

Dear Sir:

Below is a copy of a letter received from the Federal Emergency Relief Administration for North Dakota and the Public Welfare Board of North Dakota. It is sent to you to help you make correct use of whatever small income you may receive this season. If any questions arise, please consult us <u>before</u> paying debts <u>if</u> you feel you will need to apply for relief during the winter.

Very truly yours,

[Signed] Estelle Dale
County Administrator

Federal Emergency Relief Administration for North Dakota
Public Welfare Board for North Dakota
Bismarck, North Dakota

September 7, 1935

TO COUNTY RELIEF ADMINISTRATORS:

Most families will be receiving in the coming months, cash from harvest, from sale of farm produce, from allotment checks and possibly other sources.

The Relief Administration and the Board of Public Welfare advocates <u>the</u> paying of debts but <u>not</u> until the family's needs for the coming months have been met. This letter should be sent to every family which has received relief since January 1st, 1935, so that there may be no misunderstanding. Whatever money is received fron [sic] any source must be used for winter and spring needs for the family, rather than applied on debts. People who use income for the payment of debts and then apply for relief cannot receive it.

Please arrange to notify the families in your county of this matter.

Yours very truly,

E. A. Wilson
Federal Emergency Relief Administration for North Dakota
Executive Director, Public Welfare Board for North Dakota[14]

The letter was not only kind and helpful to those receiving aid but also prudent. To folks like Anders who felt a responsibility to pay his debts even when he had little or no income, the letter provided guidance in the midst of quandary. At the same time, the relief agency obviously could not use its money for anything other than emergency help and had to communicate that fact clearly to all welfare recipients.

Perhaps the ultimate in federal rescue efforts for farmers was what were called Feed and Seed Loans. Anders, and other farmers like him, had to sell every bushel harvested, and even that was not enough to support life. Hence they had to borrow money the following spring to buy enough grain to plant a crop. Farmers reduced the size of their cattle herds but even then had to borrow money to buy hay, because sufficient hay could not be grown in the horrible years of drought. The Feed and Seed Loans procured by the U.S. Department of Agriculture were the farmers' salvation.

For example, on April 25, 1937, Anders obtained an emergency crop loan from the U.S. Department of Agriculture. He borrowed $125 to purchase the seventy-five bushels of wheat needed to plant one hundred acres; $19.50 to buy thirty bushels of oats to seed twenty acres; $10 to pay for ten bushels of barley to plant ten acres; $15 to buy eight bushels of flax to seed fifteen acres; and $4 to buy one bushel of corn to plant five acres.

One government effort that was not helpful was a program to raise the price of beef by purchasing animals from farmers and slaughtering them, thus removing them from the market. One sunny summer morning in 1935 or 1936, government officials arrived on the Svendsbye farm and shot the young calves grazing in the farmyard. Watching from the north window upstairs in the house, I cried. I could not understand why my animal friends had to be killed or why all of the slaughtered animals had to be buried when meat was scarce in our household. The adult world made no sense to me. What I did not know then was that the price of beef did not rise, despite those efforts.

The state, too, tried to alleviate matters. Not only were farmers failing to pay their commercial debts, they could not pay their real estate or personal property taxes either. Letters and cards arrived at Anders' home from the county's treasurer and sheriff informing him that he was delinquent in paying his taxes. Other farmers in the state received similar notices. In 1935, the North Dakota Legislature passed a law that encouraged farmers to pay their delinquent taxes by reducing the amount of taxes owed and eliminating all interest and penalties for late payment. It reduced taxes owed from 1924 to 1930 to forty percent of what was already scaled back in 1931 to sixty percent of the original amount owed. Taxes for 1932 and 1933 were not reduced. They were generous terms, but Anders, like many others, had no money with which to respond.

The worst year of the drought for Anders and his family came in 1937. That year, northwestern North Dakota waited in vain for rain to fall. On July 5, the thermometer read 107 degrees in the shade on the Svendsbye farm. Anders decided it was too hot for both humans and animals to be out in the heat, so he canceled work for the day. But the horses needed to be watered. Three family members led the horses to a spring in a neighbor's pasture, about a mile and a half from the farmyard, so that everyone could quench their thirst. The water was ice cold.

Nothing grew that summer. There was no hay and no harvest. Anders cut some weeds—thistles—to be used later to feed the cattle, but even that yielded less than half the usual wagon load. Hay had to be purchased to carry the animals through the winter, and, with no income to buy as much as was really needed, hay had to be rationed. The total crop failure of 1937 was devastating. The number of animals on the farm had declined drastically from the previous decade because of the poor pastures and the need to buy hay. The number of horses dropped from what had been a high of eleven to five that year. The number of cattle dropped from a high of forty to just under a dozen. On the 1938 chattel mortgage, the cattle numbered eight. That year even the twenty chickens were listed.

The animals also suffered the consequences of the drought. For them there was less grass, less hay, less oats, and even less straw. Difficulties developed in part because the horses were aging, but also because there were often no oats with which to supplement their diet. Normally, horses working in the fields were fed oats at least twice a day, but some years that was not possible or they got smaller quantities. Near the end of the 1939 harvest season, the oldest of the four horses pulling the binder simply played out. She stopped in the middle of the field, bringing the binder to a halt. She did not move for several minutes, as she swayed from side to side, until she had rested. After waiting for a while, Anders unhitched the horses from the binder and was able to drive them home. The remaining days of the harvest had to be significantly shortened and the horses given long rest periods after each round in order to complete the harvest.

Finally, in 1940, things started to change, and 1941 was a year of rejoicing. Several times in June 1941 it rained steadily for a few days in a row. The crops were heavy and thick, the yields were excellent, and the price of wheat was improving. The federal government paid farmers a higher price for their grain than could be obtained on

Anders Svendsbye driving a binder cutting grain in the field in front of the Svendsbye house. Jean Svendsbye is paying her father a visit in 1946.

the market and stored it in farm granaries rather than in commercial elevators. With income on the rise, some farmers declared bankruptcy, then purchased new tractors and combines to harvest the crop.

Refusing to declare bankruptcy and insisting on paying his debts, Anders continued to use horses and his old binder. The bundles sped through the binder. There were so many they formed rows only a few feet apart. When the bundles had been put into shocks to dry, they looked especially beautiful when one saw them against the morning or evening sun.

Anders began to repay his debts in 1940, when the crops began to improve and there was money. He sent $77.82 and $113.46 to the Williams County treasurer to begin to pay his delinquent taxes for 1934 and 1937. With a bumper crop in 1941, his pace of debt payments quickened—and continued for twenty-one years, until every penny owed had been paid, with interest.

For example, on November 28, 1941, Anders sent $47.35 for delinquent taxes to the Williams County Sheriff. The following day, he sent payments of $281.46 and $210.33 to the Williams County Treasurer to pay for delinquent taxes on his land for the years 1935-1939. On November 28, he sent $765 to the Federal Land Bank, after sending them a check for $350 a week earlier. On December 20, he repaid a February

17, 1930, demand note of $150 plus interest from the Citizens Bank of Wildrose and a September 17, 1937, note for $119.53 plus interest.

July 1952 marked a significant achievement for Anders. He completed repaying one of his $2,000 Federal Land Bank loans, plus interest. The bank returned the note—now stamped "paid"—and enclosed a cordial letter, dated July 21, 1952, that stated, in part:

> With the recent completion of final payment on your land bank loan you have become one of the many who have successfully used the services of this cooperative loan system. We are happy that the bank and your national farm loan association have had the opportunity to be of service to you. We are especially pleased that you have attained the goal of full clearance of the mortgage obligation. This accomplishment must certainly be a matter of considerable satisfaction to you.[15]

Ten years later, the final $2,000 loan, for which Anders had mortgaged his homestead, was also paid in full, with interest.

Some of Anders' friends and neighbors must have been puzzled why he did not file for bankruptcy in the 1940s, as many of them did. Released from the burden of debt, they were free to use their increased income to buy more land as well as new machinery. Some of those neighbors became prosperous and drove new and expensive cars. When Anders was asked why he didn't declare bankruptcy, he said simply, "I owe the money." He used his money to pay his debts, while continuing to farm with horses and drive his 1929 Model A Ford. For Anders, this was a moral decision.

Despite the hardships that accompanied life during the drought and Depression, Anders never expressed reservations about having emigrated. Nor did he ever express a desire to travel to Norway, even for a short visit. Gudrun, too, never indicated anything but support for their joint enterprise. Both were content to be where they were, however severe the economic hardships.

CHAPTER 6

Family Life

The Context

Anders and Gudrun Svendsbye were, in many senses, typical Norwegian immigrants of the first half of the twentieth century. Their roles were well defined by the society of the time. The husband was the head of the house and expected to be waited on—that is, to have meals and coffee ready when he was, to have his clothes washed and mended as needed, and to have his bed ready for sleeping each night. The wife did all the housework and helped outside with farm work when necessary. Life focused primarily on work. Physical work. In typical fashion, Anders was the undisputed head of the house. He made the final decision on all matters, unless he chose not to. He was full of energy and liked to work outside the house, but he never lifted a finger to do anything approaching work inside the house, though he did regularly make coffee the first thing in the morning after he had put on his workday clothes. He lit a fire in the cookstove, boiled water, and put a modest amount of coffee into the small aluminum coffee pot—enough to provide him and Gudrun each with two cups of weak coffee—which they drank without cream although Anders usually added a lump of sugar and perhaps a cookie, dunking both into his drink.

During the morning coffee period, Anders and Gudrun often spoke Norwegian with each other, even though they were firm in their conviction that English should be the family language. Despite Anders' concurrence on that point, in one real sense he preferred Norwegian because it was easier for him, although he almost always spoke English to the children. He spoke English with a brogue and regularly made a number of grammatical errors. Gudrun preferred English, which she spoke without a brogue and generally correctly, except for such standard mix-ups with lie and lay, saw and seen, and the like. Those errors simply put her in line with other immigrants speaking English. But when the two of them wanted to have a heart-to-heart conversation with morning coffee or when they did not want to be understood by listening family, they spoke Norwegian. However, several of the siblings knew some Norwegian so, even when they could not understand everything said, they often were able to figure out the general sense of the parental discussion.

Gudrun was responsible for all the housework. The children helped her as they grew older, but even after they were old enough to sweep floors, make beds, and wash and wipe dishes, she did most of the cooking, baking, clothes washing, ironing, and mending. In the first two decades of their marriage, Gudrun did a considerable amount of farm work as well. She helped milk the cows twice daily and sometimes carried pails of water into the barn to give to the calves. Taking care of the chickens—feeding them, collecting the eggs, and nesting them in the spring—was also her responsibility. During the summer she helped with the haying and harvest. I am told that in 1930, she carried me to the field and laid me on a blanket in the shade of a specially-constructed shock of grain. At the time she was nursing me.

The house on the farm had four rooms. It had only three when Anders and Lina moved into it. After Lina's death, when Elling and Johanna were staying with Anders to help take care of Margaret, Anders added a fourteen-by-ten-foot bedroom. Oral tradition has it that Anders was planning to build a two-story addition with two bedrooms, but that the brothers got into an argument, resulting in the building of only one additional room. In that bedroom, Gudrun gave birth to seven of her nine children whom her mother, Gjertru, delivered.

Albert tells about coming home from school around four in the afternoon on May 26, 1930, and hearing my first cries. Anders was not at home. He was in the field. He probably reasoned that he could not do anything at home since Gjertru was in charge, so he might as well not waste time and get on with the seeding. In any event, only Gudrun and Gjertru were present at birth. Hence, when births occurred, the older children were exposed only to the sounds behind the curtain, never to the sights, except for some preparations which may have taken place in the kitchen.

For all the events that occurred in that house, it was very small and crowded. Even with a fourth room, the house provided only 820 square feet for a family that sometimes had ten of their twelve members at home at the same time. And for all purposes other than sleeping, the family lived and worked in the kitchen and living room. In that ten-by-twelve-foot kitchen, Gudrun cooked, baked, washed her laundry and dishes, and served coffee and lunches two or three times a day. On the one side of the room stood cabinets and a table on which food was prepared and dishes washed. Underneath the table were cream cans for storing water. On the other side was the kitchen stove, space for storing coal, a wooden box used as a washstand, and the cream separator. A trap door had been cut in the middle of the floor to provide an entrance to the cellar. It was a small, dark space used to store potatoes, other vegetables, and canned goods. For light, one needed to carry a flashlight or a small lamp. In 1952, after the house was wired for electricity, a refrigerator filled a niche. Gudrun was a neat person, and she worked hard to keep the house tidy. She swept and washed the floors every day with the kitchen as her biggest challenge. The room was hard to keep clean, in part because it opened directly to the outside, without the benefit of an entryway. That door, the only entrance to the house, was the perfect way for everyone who entered to soil the kitchen floor, which often needed to be washed several times a day.

In the fourteen-by-twenty-foot living room, the family gathered daily to converse, eat, read, listen to the radio, do the homework required for school, laugh, argue, and sometimes sleep for want of other space. Its main piece of furniture was a round oak dining table, with chairs that did not match. On the table stood a kerosene lamp, the only source of light after dark. There was also a sofa that could be made into a bed that the girls used and a coal-burning stove called "the heater," which warmed the entire house, except the kitchen. Scattered around the house were wooden chairs and a wooden rocker. On the walls hung the telephone, a calendar, some framed poems, pictures of rural scenes and an imposing picture of Anders as a young man.

At the north end of the living room was a bedroom, used by Anders and Gudrun, except when additional space was needed for some of the children. A wide door separated the two rooms. Initially, plans were to separate the rooms with double French doors, but that proved to be too expensive so a curtain was hung instead to provide a semblance of separation and privacy. However, most of the time the curtain was held aside with ties so that the door was essentially open all the time. The bed stood at an angle facing the northwest corner, dominating the small room. To the left was a window under which a sewing machine stood. Next to it along the south wall was a tall, wooden wardrobe in which Anders and

Gudrun stored most of their clothes. To the right of the bed was a window alongside of which was a dresser with a cracked mirror and a unit that had special space for a commode. Along the east wall was the space used for a second bed, or, in its absence, more storage compartments. In the southeast corner stood the washing machine that was wheeled out to the kitchen promptly every Monday morning at 7:00 a.m. There was no lamp in the room. At night, light came from the living room through the large door; otherwise, flashlights were used.

A steep stairway without railings led to the upstairs which was divided into two rooms. The larger space provided a bedroom for the boys, and the smaller space was used for storage. In the bedroom were two beds with straw-filled mattresses and a chest of four drawers used by all of the siblings to store underclothing, handkerchiefs, and the like. On top of the chest was a small kerosene lamp that was a favorite of mine because even though the light was dim, it provided me with enough light to read at night while standing. All the boys' clothes and some of the girls' were hung on two large brackets bolted to the wall and covered with white sheets. The rest of the girls' clothes were hung on a six foot wall-to-wall wire in the storage room. Behind the clothes, there was a cramped space with shelves on which less-used items were stored. On the other side of the small room was more storage space for a couple of trunks and additional shelving, together with a three-foot-square wooden box containing the flour Gudrun used for baking. Jackets, coats, and caps used for school and everyday wear by the children were hung on long nails which lined the narrow stairway.

The farmstead had seven unpainted structures by the time most of the children were born: a house, a barn, a chicken house, a one-car garage, a coal shed, Anders' homestead shack (moved from his homestead), and a cook-car. I yearned for a large white house and a large red barn, which some neighbors had, but that was not to be.

The barn was forty feet long, and wide enough for stalls to ring both sides, leaving a ten-foot area in the middle with eight-foot sliding doors on both ends. Forty feet provided enough space for five eight-foot stalls for the horses on one side and six six-foot stalls for the cattle on the other side, leaving just enough space for a four-foot wide grain bin to store the ground oats used to feed the horses. On the side of the barn where the horses stood was the hay shed, a space ten feet wide running the entire length of the barn. Entrance to the hay shed was through one of

The Svendsbye farmyard.

the horse stalls used only for one horse. The barn leaned so badly to one side it eventually had to be propped up with a telephone pole. Because it leaned so much, the door did not close properly, and during the winter snow had to be piled against the door to plug the gap and help keep out the wind. The roof sloped slightly and had been covered with tar paper. As the tar paper wore out, flax straw was put on top of the roof to help keep heat in the barn during the winter. In the summer when it rained, the roof leaked like a sieve. We had to use shovels to scoop up the dirty water into buckets which we carried out and dumped down the hill. By the late 1950s the situation was so bad that the barn was pulled into the middle of a field and burned.

The ten-by-sixteen chicken house was divided into two parts. The larger part was used by the chickens, and the smaller part by a hog or two. Three two-by-fours running the length of one side of the chicken house provided enough space for all the chickens to roost at one time. Two boxes were bolted to the top of one wall adjacent to the roosts, to provide spaces in which the hens could lay their eggs and for easy access from the roosts to the nests. To provide warmth, the building was covered by bales of flax straw. From the time the weather got cold in the fall until the snow melted in the spring, the chickens remained in the chicken house where they were fed and watered daily. In the spring, Gudrun placed three or four hens on nests with about eight eggs each which netted a bit over thirty chicks. They were kept in a fenced area until they were old enough to maneuver around the yard. About half of them were roosters. When ready to be eaten, it was my assignment to catch each bird and chop off its head. Also in the spring, a small pig or two was purchased and sometimes kept in an outside pen until butchering time.

Four other buildings provided a variety of uses. The garage, which was barely large enough for the Model A, disintegrated badly and was torn down about the same time as the barn. Next to the garage stood a twelve-by-twelve building that was used for storing coal until it was co-opted for a granary. Anders' homestead shack was placed on two three-by-sixes and pulled across the fields by four horses to a spot about 200 feet east of the house and was used either to store coal or grain, depending on the need. After Albert took over the farm, he moved the shack down near the barn and used it as a combined well house and tool shed. The cook car, originally used to cook meals for the threshing crews when Anders and a neighbor operated a threshing

Anders and Edward, having shoveled out the doors of the garage and the chicken house in the late '40s.

rig, became a space to store tools as well as frozen meat and fish during the winter. During the summer, it also served as a place for the younger siblings to play. With the exception of Anders' homestead shack, which is the only original building left standing on the farm, all the other buildings deteriorated to the point where they too met their fate by fire.

The Texture of Family Life

Despite the obvious poverty reflected by the farmstead, the family did not usually think of themselves as poor. Anders and Gudrun were good parents. They were even-handed in dealing with their children, all of whom were well disciplined. All had to obey their parents, without talking back. All were expected to behave decently and in a socially accepted way. All ate whatever was provided for them without complaint. They were expected to speak clearly, without shouting. They were expected to keep themselves and their clothes as clean and neat as possible. As soon as anything became even the slightest bit soiled, Gudrun washed it. Torn clothing was mended immediately. None of the children were given special treatment. All were expected to be good students (and they were), to do their schoolwork on time, and to read as much as possible. Fights among the siblings were few.

While the parents gave priority to feeding, clothing, and keeping the children clean, attention was also given to behavior, character building, and especially learning. The public school sent home report cards for each child every six weeks. Anders in particular studied them carefully. If achievements were below expectation or poor conduct was reported, he brought the matter to the attention of the erring child in a personal and forceful manner. No one could fail to know what was expected.

Almost all of the family's clothing was ordered from the Montgomery Ward and Sears Roebuck catalogs. With economic conditions what they were, Gudrun ordered both materials and patterns from the catalogs and sewed many of the dresses and underclothing worn by herself and the girls. The younger children wore clothes that had been outgrown by the older ones. In the case of the boys, blue denim jeans or overalls were ordered from the catalog. The allotment was generally one new pair of overalls and one or two new shirts for each boy, purchased at the beginning of each school year. The shirts and overalls were often patched in order to be worn for more than one school year. But everything was clean.

Shoes really had to be worn out before they could be discarded. When holes were worn completely through the sole of a shoe, the cardboard back of a writing tablet was cut to the appropriate size and put inside the shoe to provide some protection for the foot. When cardboard was not available, the daily newspaper was used. One year Albert had to wear unmatched shoes to school in order to have two shoes without holes.

While it was necessary to wear patched clothing and on occasion unmatched shoes, one did from time to time require a haircut. Gudrun cut the girls' hair with a pair of scissors. The boys received free haircuts from their brother-in-law, Margaret's husband, Gilmer, whose clipper was so dull it pulled hairs. When he was not available, another neighbor did the task for a dime. A few years later, it was necessary to get a professional job at the Wildrose barbershop for 25 cents.

Keeping an eye on the need for haircuts, ordering clothes from the catalog, and seeing that everyone had shoes to wear were among Gudrun's simpler tasks. Five days a week—and sometimes six—she baked four or five loaves of bread each day. When the children came home from school, they always had fresh bread to eat, often without butter, but generally with peanut butter. She made countless lunches each day. Two lunches accompanied Anders and Albert each when they worked in the fields. Each child carried his or her lunch to school in a half-gallon tin pail that had once held Karo syrup. Lunches generally consisted of two slices of bread with jelly or peanut butter on them. Sometimes the county welfare office had extra cheese they distributed to families in need, which Gudrun also used for sandwiches.

For the first twenty years of her married life, Gudrun washed all the clothes and bedding by hand. Since there was no running water in the house, the water had to be carried in from outside barrels. It was heated in a tub or boiler placed on the hottest spot on the top of the cook-stove. Washing everything by hand meant that each piece was rubbed with soap against a washboard. Since water was scarce, the same water was used several times for both washing and rinsing. Sheets, pillowcases, and other white items were boiled on the cookstove. On June 6, 1938, an event occurred that considerably lightened the laundry process. Anders and Gudrun went to Ray and bought a Norge clothes washer for $105. With no electricity on the farm, it was powered by a gasoline engine. To keep the fumes from polluting the air in the rest of the house, the south kitchen window was opened so that the exhaust pipe could extend outside.

During the warm months, the clothes were hung on lines of thick wire strung between a telephone pole and the house. Who washed clothes on what day was a perennial subject of conversation in the community. It became a matter of pride for Gudrun to demonstrate to the neighbors that she got her clothes out on the line before the neighbors did. She just had to have her first load of clothes on the line by 8:00 a.m.—and usually did. During the winter, everything had to be dried inside the house, which meant in the living room. There was so much moisture in the air from the drying clothes that the living room walls and ceiling had to be wiped dry at the end of the day.

Gudrun ironed the clothes and other laundry in the living room the following day. She used heavy flatirons—specially shaped pieces of iron that were heated on the top of the kitchen stove. As each iron cooled, it was taken to the stove and exchanged for a hot one. While she was ironing, one could often hear her singing her favorite hymns, such as "What a Friend We Have in Jesus," "Sweet Hour of Prayer," and "Jesus Loves Me."

A regular visitor to the Svendsbye home was the "Watkins Man," a traveling salesman who bumped along the poorly graded roads in his old Ford to call on his customers. There was considerable interest to see the large variety of items he carried in his display case. Gudrun regularly purchased certain basic staples for the family, most of which were cold remedies ranging from a variety of cough syrups and cough drops to such a standard necessity as Vick's VapoRub®. There was also Vaseline®, which was the household's most important healing medication for burns and cuts. In addition, there was a host of spices. The "Watkins Man" provided genuine service for rural folk because his visits saved them from the need to shop for those items in town. Besides, he sold them at a low price.

There was a genuine rhythm to life on the farm. Meals were served promptly at 6:30 a.m., noon, and 6:30 p.m. Everyone was expected to be at the table every day. On special occasions it was assumed I would say a table prayer in Norwegian. I cannot recall now—if I ever knew— why this particular honor or task was mine. After I left home this duty fell to younger siblings. During the Depression, when there were not enough chairs, wooden boxes—often apple crates—were substituted. Conversation was encouraged. Those who were rude were reprimanded. Discussions centered on what was going on in the local community as well as in the state, nation, and world.

The family subscribed to several newspapers and magazines. Anders subscribed to the *Decorah Posten*, *Normanden*, and *Scandinaven*. Both parents were sensitive to the need for English newspapers. The *Williston Daily Herald* met that need for a while, but in the 1940s it was supplemented by the *Fargo Forum* and *Grit*. There were two farm magazines, *The Farmer* and *Capper's Farmer*, and of course the *Wildrose Mixer*, a weekly paper that concentrated on local news. Because of high family interest in the political process, Anders purchased a Zenith battery-operated radio in 1940 so that the family could regularly listen to the daily news and the speeches of President Roosevelt and his Republican opponent that year, Wendell Wilkie, as well as candidates for other state and national offices. On the night before the elections, the airwaves were filled with politicians outlining their views and making their appeals to the people.

All members of the family were expected to listen to the daily newscasts, special reports, and political speeches. If it was necessary for anyone to speak during those times, conversations were to be kept in low tones and as brief as possible. Anders himself sometimes broke the rule by interjecting, "Dumhet!" (Norwegian for foolishness) in reaction to some notion argued by a politician. After the broadcasts, the radio was turned off, and discussions and work ensued. Only occasionally were family members allowed to listen to music or other entertainment programs. Exceptions included a couple of afternoon soap operas, such as *Ma Perkins*, which Anders liked, and a few evening programs such as

Fibber McGee and Molly, the *Grand Ole Opry,* and *Your Hit Parade.* Two broadcast events regularly listened to were the play-by-play accounts of the world heavyweight boxing matches in New York's Madison Square Garden and the annual regional and state basketball tournaments.

Politics was an important subject for discussion. Anders was a loyal fan of William Langer, who was governor of North Dakota from 1933 to 1934 and again from 1937 to 1939, before he was elected to the U.S. Senate in 1940. Langer was a controversial figure in the state, but Anders defended him as a friend of the farmer and repeatedly made clear to the family why, in his judgment, Langer deserved support. Gudrun quietly disagreed and in some elections voted for Langer's opponent. Langer, a Nonpartisan League Republican, clearly fought for the farmer. As governor he proclaimed, as Robinson describes, "a moratorium on all debts, . . . soon restricting [the state banks] to forbid foreclosures only on real property being farmed by the owner."[1] Langer called out the National Guard to stop the sheriffs' sales of land that had been foreclosed. They were bold and significant actions. But Roosevelt appeared to be equally pro-farmer. As a result of programs he initiated, millions of dollars poured into North Dakota, without which Anders would never have survived.

Most of the children became staunch supporters of the Republican Party, some actively. Only three became Democrats. Anders was generally critical of everything President Roosevelt did or attempted to do. Gudrun's voting record was more flexible.

Anders' reaction to Roosevelt and Langer seemed to be contradictory to me as a teenager. Both appeared to be friends of the farmer who worked hard on the farmers' behalf. But in supporting Langer and opposing Roosevelt, Anders was typical of many North Dakota farmers. Actually, Anders was quite conservative. Socialist notions were popular in parts of rural Norway around the beginning of the twentieth century, and many Norwegian immigrants brought those convictions to North Dakota and other places where they settled. As Robinson points out, Williams and Ward counties in the northwestern part of the state helped the Socialist Party reach its highest-ever peak of about eight percent of the statewide vote, in 1912.[2] But Anders was no socialist. The closest he came to espousing similar ideas was in his support of the Nonpartisan League, which early established its long affiliation with the Republican Party. Whatever his reasons, Anders remained staunchly Republican, with the exception of his support for Quentin Burdick. In 1956, the Nonpartisan League formally moved into the Democratic Party. In that year Burdick was that party's unsuccessful candidate for the U.S. House. But he won a House seat in 1958, then a U.S. Senate seat in 1960, with Anders' blessing.

The biggest irony in Anders' life was his ambivalence toward government aid in all its forms, despite the fact he was a recipient of it. His independence and his basic sense of dignity seem to have inwardly revolted against the very programs that kept him and his family alive. He accepted relief because it was necessary, but it was an insult to his pride. According to his basic values, he was responsible for providing everything his family needed. Accepting aid bent his core values and in turn fed his determination to pay back every cent he owed. It may have even contributed to some of his moodiness. According to Elwyn Robinson, this apparent contradiction plagued other North Dakota immigrant farmers as well. "Farmers were individualists," he wrote, "each running his own enterprise. Aid and direction from the federal government accentuated North Dakota's dependent status, an unhappy outcome for many touchy North Dakotans."

A surprising fact arises about government aid in North Dakota to people in need. Aid began early among the immigrants, long before the New Deal swept the land. Caring for the neighbor was a value immigrants espoused in the kind of culture they developed, despite the fact some were inwardly alienated. Anders, for example, believed he should help others, and he did. It was accepting aid for himself that created the inner tension he seems to have experienced. Early on, the minutes of both the county and the township boards recorded instances when boards wrestled with an issue they had not anticipated in the new land—poverty. The minutes do not reflect arguments about whether government had a responsibility to help people, the question focused on was how much money should be used. And the community of immigrant citizens, of which Anders was an active part, demanded that something be done.

As early as February 9, 1910, the Williams County Commissioners received a petition signed by a pastor and thirty-four other persons about a neighbor said to be "in sore distress financially after having done all in his power to supply himself with sufficient funds to carry him through." After discussion, the board voted to send the needy man $15.00. One week later, the board received a petition from a woman who described herself as "97 years old," and "the first white woman in Williams County" who had no means of support because she had lost all her property in litigation.

Following deliberation, the board voted unanimously to instruct the county auditor to pay the woman $10.00 per month "until ordered stopped."

Not all requests were approved. On March 8, 1922, the Big Meadow Township Board voted down a request for $106.15 to pay doctor bills and related items for one of its citizens. The board declined because "after making a thorough investigation" they found "the party of the principal hereof in fair circumstances and by far better than others in similar circumstances." Similarly, in the spring of 1937, in response to a request to pay doctor bills for Gjertru Birkelo, the board declined saying, "Due to reasons to which the township has no control, no definite action was taken." What those reasons were was not spelled out. The point is that in the prairie culture which the citizens had formed, requests for assistance were made; the boards deliberated and helped some, but not all.

In the mid-1930s, the responsibility for relief and welfare was taken over by the national, state, and county governments. The New Deal required states and counties to administer some of the new programs. Accordingly, the North Dakota state legislature established the Public Welfare Board early in 1935, and on October 10 of the same year, the Williams County Welfare Board was organized. Anders had reservations about both moves, yet he and the Birkelo family received aid from them. The elected representatives worked hard for their constituencies. At the county level, they lobbied for WPA (Works Progress Adminsitration) projects. At the township level, "coal grants" were established to help residents with their heating bills. The county decided who would get the grants. The township then set aside funds to pay people to work for them. This meant that if someone needed coal for the winter, that person could apply to the county for a grant, and, if approved, apply to the township board to allocate enough hours of work to pay for the grant. All in all, the community ethos set the wheels of government in motion to take care of needy citizens. The matter of aid remained an ambivalent matter for Anders to the end of his life. The principle was discussed around the dinner table.

The household also vigorously discussed events leading up to the entry of the United States into World War II. Anders was initially critical of President Roosevelt for trying to prepare for war, although Germany's invasion of Norway in the spring of 1940 gave him a different perspective. After the attack on Pearl Harbor, he faithfully supported the war effort. Nevertheless, he basically remained opposed to war as a means of settling disputes among nations. Asked why, he repeatedly said, "War never settled anything." When two young men in a neighboring county declared themselves conscientious objectors, Anders was sympathetic, although his own sons were not.

In discussions about the war, there were conversations about why people in Germany, Italy, and Japan would support their leaders. But there was little expressed hostility toward the German or Italian people. Negative references tended not to be directly toward Germans but to "the Nazis." Eisenhower's oft-repeated reference to Hitler or the Nazis as "the German" did not catch on. The Italians were largely ignored, but the Japanese were another matter. Everybody in the community remembered Pearl Harbor, and, fairly or not, most people held it against the entire nation of Japan, not only its leaders. In our home, as well as in the filling stations, elevators, or general stores where men of the community gathered and visited, the people of Japan were regularly and derisively referred to as "Japs," often with expletives. One can only speculate about whether such attitudes were affected by the fact that some neighbors in the community were of German heritage but none were from Japan.

The events marking both the entry of the United States into the war and its climactic ending are etched in the collective memories of the entire family. Many remember exactly where they were when the attack on Pearl Harbor was announced on the radio. Sitting on the floor, next to the stove, I was concerned about whether Albert would now be drafted into the armed forces and, if so, might he be killed. That horrifying thought frightened me. The entire family listened in silence. The end of the war is equally clear in memory. The family heard the announcement about the dropping of the first atom bomb on Hiroshima during a noon hour news broadcast. Driving out to the hay field after the noon break, Albert said, "This changes the world forever." I asked why. "Because this kind of power never existed before," he replied, ending the conversation.

The Quality of Life

While subjects under discussion in the home ranged from war to weather, there was almost no discussion of religion, faith, or theology. The family talked about events that occurred in the churches but not about what churches were alleged to believe, even though everyone in the family attended all worship events and whatever else was scheduled at Grong Church.

Despite their near silence regarding Christian teaching and practice, Anders and Gudrun gave a strong indication to their children that the church, and by implication, faith, was important. Exactly why was never stated or discussed. One was to go to church to listen and learn. Hence attendance was a top priority.

There were no English-language religious documents in the house—no Bible, hymnal, catechism, prayer book, or devotional readings. There was an unspoken creed that Christianity equaled a particular kind of morality, sternly espoused by Anders. It was not a morality that lifted up love and justice, but rather one that emphasized a kind of personal denial: no drinking of alcohol, no dancing, no sex outside marriage, and no smoking, although at one time Anders himself smoked quite heavily. The closest thing to a ritual in the home was an occasional table prayer. There were no evening devotions or bedtime prayers led by the parents. If or when Anders and Gudrun prayed, there were no witnesses, only to Gudrun's ironing day hymns about prayer. They may have prayed silently, but if so, there were no references to it among the family. Even prayers for rain were never a matter of family conversation. Drought, like cold weather, was simply accepted as a given, about which there was nothing to do.

Despite the usual reticence to speak about matters of faith, one conversation with my mother about death stands out in memory. The occasion was the first community death I can recall, some time prior to my starting school. I asked my mother, "How do people die?" She replied, "God calls them home." I shuddered. I liked my neighbors and did not want them to disappear. I thought, how could God be so mean? I did not like God. But I did not share those thoughts with my mother. Gudrun and Anders were rather matter-of-fact about death. Both mourned in obvious ways when a death occurred in the family, but if their mourning continued for any length of time, it was not visible and not part of family conversations. Apart from firmly held morals, faith for Anders and Gudrun was the uncomplaining acceptance of the inevitable.

One of the events the Svendsbye siblings did observe and discuss quietly was the romance between our oldest sister Alice and Art Vatne, who was also the brother of our sister Margaret Vatne's husband Gilmer. Alice graduated from high school in 1937. She remained at home the following year because there was no money to attend college and there were no jobs in the community, except for occasional days at various farms when there were special needs such as baking bread or washing clothes. She did spend considerable time with her grandparents, Thor and Gjertru Birkelo, with whom she could speak Norwegian. There were no crops that year so there was not even the opportunity to help with feeding the threshers. But sometime during the year, she and Art decided to marry. Those were hard times, even for courtship. Art did the best he could do. He did not own a car, not even a team of horses. But he owned skis. In the winter of 1937-1938, he would strap on his skis to travel the five miles across country from the Vatne farm to the Svendsbye home with his guitar slung over his shoulder. With only four rooms in the Svendsbye home, there was no possibility for privacy, so Alice and Art did two things. They sat in the corner of the davenport holding hands and talked with each other in very low tones while the younger brothers and sisters strained to hear what was said. After a while, Art picked up his guitar and strummed on it while he entertained the entire family by singing, mainly gospel songs. Soon there was a wedding.

Most weddings at that time were held in private homes. Only one wedding was held in Grong church while Olav Lin was pastor, although a few were held in his office. A surprisingly large number were held in the home of a justice of the peace. The three oldest Svendsbye daughters were married in each of those locations. Margaret was married in the Lutheran Free Church parsonage in Wildrose; Alice was married at home on the farm; and Lillian was married by a justice of the peace in Bozeman, Montana. Alice was thus the only one whose wedding was observed by the entire family. I remember it well. It was on June 1, 1938. Pastor George Melby of Trinity Lutheran Church in Hamlet officiated. The Lutheran Free Church had no official wedding liturgy, so Pastor Melby simply stood at the west window of the family living room and motioned Alice and Art to take their places facing him. The attendants, Albert Svendsbye and Helen Vatne, stood behind them. The wedding ceremony then began with a few comments by Pastor Melby, followed by a free prayer and a song, "I Love You Truly," sung by three younger sisters of the bride: Lillian, Gladys, and Ida. Pastor Melby then preached for what seemed like a long time, especially if one's instructions were to sit without moving. Then the pastor sang "God Will Take Care of You," prayed again, and then asked the families to join him in the Lord's Prayer. That ended the ceremony; there was no benediction. Pastor Melby simply congratulated the newlyweds after which everyone went out into the farm yard and gathered in front of the tree field for a photo. This was followed by a light luncheon of Jello salad and wedding cake with coffee or nectar, and, of course, more visiting.

One of the fun things community members did for their friends who got married was to stage what was called a shivaree. This was planned as a surprise. A short caravan of cars made their way, after dark, without lights, across prairie trails to the home of the newly married couple. Alice and Art were living that summer with his parents on their farm. The caravan crossed the hills to the south of the farm house, and, when close enough to the house but still out of sight, two of the neighbor men walked the rest of the way to the house through the darkness and knocked on the porch door. When it was clear that both Alice and Art were there, the men signaled the rest of the caravan with a flash light that all was clear and they were to come. With lights on and horns blaring, the caravan entered the Vatne farm yard and surrounded the house with their cars. Alice and Art were invited to get into a small trailer that was hitched to one of the cars. With the newlyweds in tow and the horns blaring, the caravan set out across the prairie hills and wound up at another neighbor's home where they stopped, as planned, for ice cream, coffee, and cake to celebrate the wedding. The couple was escorted home with the same flair and personalized attention.

One other wedding celebration of great importance to the Svends-bye family was the twenty-fifth wedding anniversary of Anders and Gudrun, celebrated in December 1943 in Grong Lutheran Church. Because there were so few such celebrations in a church, it is not clear why their celebration was held there, unless it was because a neighbor couple had observed their anniversary that way. Since it was in the church, Pastor Lin was scheduled to preside. A few nights before the event, Anders expressed some curiosity at the dinner table about what Lin would say about him and Gudrun. Lin was a straight

Anders and Gudrun Svendsbye on the twenty-fifth wedding anniversary.

shooter that day. Nothing was said about the celebrants' glowing faith. Instead, he made a simple, accurate observation: Whenever something was scheduled in the church, one could always count on the Svendsbyes to be there. That was satisfactory to Anders because he always emphasized attendance. After the program, coffee and lunch were served by the women of the congregation from the food they brought with them to the ceremony. There were no flowers except for a paper corsage worn by Gudrun who had hay-fever and could not tolerate fresh flowers.

Birthdays were always celebrated. With ten children in the family, we celebrated often. There was always a cake, usually white angel food with white frosting. The cake was always baked on the birthday and never served to the family until evening. That meant the cake was fresh to serve any neighbors who came by in the afternoon, usually when Anders and Gudrun celebrated their birthdays. Some neighbors regularly brought a cake for the birthday guest, while others did not. The entire family gathered in the evening and sang "Happy Birthday" before eating the rest of the cake. There were no birthday gifts until during World War II, when gifts were limited to one gift per birthday child.

There was an amazing continuity from season to season and year to year in the life of the family. The day usually began at 5:00 a.m. Anders, who normally awakened before the alarm clock rang, would rise, dress, and kindle fires in the two stoves. As small children, we would wait until the living room had warmed sufficiently, then dash into the room in our long johns and gather around the stove to dress. After we were old enough to help with the morning chores in the barn, Anders would come to the foot of the stairs and say, "Er dere väken gutter?" ("Are you awake, boys?") The question was posed only once. Albert and I were usually downstairs, washed, dressed, and ready to go to the barn by the time Anders finished his first cup of coffee.

During the winter, Albert always lit the lantern to take to the barn. The horses began neighing when they heard the barn door open, so they were fed first, followed by the cattle. The cows were then milked by hand. We returned to the house to operate the cream separator. That involved getting a good grip on the handle with one hand, putting the separator in gear, and turning the handle in a circular motion. The object was to get the gears going fast enough to twirl the disks of the separator with sufficient speed so they could separate the cream from the skim milk, each flowing through spouts into separate containers. Following the separation, most of the skim milk went to feed the calves or hogs, with a full pitcher saved for Anders who appreciated warm skim milk, which his children did not.

The cream was put into a five gallon cream can in the cellar to be kept as cool as possible. Often, because there was no refrigeration, the cream soured so it was useful only for making butter. When the can was full, the proper address label was wired to the can and it was taken to Hamlet in the back seat of the Model A or in the sleigh box during the winter, left in the depot to be picked up by the next Great Northern train going east. Normally, the cream was sent to the Farmer's Union Creamery in Williston, so the Great Northern would take the cream can to Stanley where another Great Northern train on the main line going west would pick it up and bring it to the Williston Railroad Station. There a truck from the Farmer's Union would pick it up and haul it to the creamery. After examining the cream for things such as butterfat content, the creamery would classify it, empty the cream into a big vat with other cream, wash the can, write a check to Anders, mail the check, and return the cream can to Hamlet by the same route it had come to them.

Taking care of the milk was an important process and done with great care. It was also an enjoyable way to begin the day. When the part of the process we did in the kitchen was completed, we sat down to breakfast, during which we listened to fifteen minutes of national news, followed by a local musician who sang familiar hymns and Western music. The breakfast included either oatmeal, cream of wheat, cold cereal, or two slices of bread toasted on the top of the kitchen-stove, with coffee for those who wanted it. After breakfast Anders and Albert left for the barn, where they groomed the horses and gave water to all the animals. The siblings got ready to go to school and helped Gudrun by washing the dishes, making the beds, and sweeping the floor.

During the growing season, Anders and Albert harnessed the horses so that they could all start work in the fields at 7:00. After two hours of work, they enjoyed a lunch of jelly or peanut butter sandwiches and coffee—either carried to the field by one of the siblings or by the men when they went to the field. At 11:45 they unhitched the horses in order to drive them home by noon. After the horses were given water and fed, dinner was promptly served.

During the half hour used for eating, the family listened attentively to two fifteen-minute news programs of mostly national and international news. One of the regular news commentators at the time was H. B. Kaltenborn of NBC. Following dinner and news, Anders would lie down on the sofa in the living room, put a newspaper over his face, and take a fifteen-minute nap. At 1:00, he went back to the fields after a cup of coffee and a cookie. Afternoon coffee and lunch came at 3:30. By 6:15 the horses were home and ready to be unharnessed.

The cattle too required attention. During the dry years there was not always enough grass in the pasture for them to eat, so they had to be driven to land in the nearby school section in order to find for them enough grass for grazing. When let out of the pasture, they had to be herded so that they did not stray into a neighbor's fields. Albert and Gladys did most of that work, including chasing the cattle to a nearby spring or to a slough with water in it.

The pasture fences were also casualties. The wooden posts rotted. With nothing to replace them, long stretches of fence had only a few posts to hold the wire in place. The cattle found it easy under those circumstances to break through the fences and head to the neighbors' fields. When that happened, the siblings were summoned to round up the erring cattle and return them to their proper pastures. To try to prevent the cattle from breaking out, heavy wooden yokes were put around their necks. While that was helpful, some of the cattle were nevertheless able to break out from time to time and cause trouble. One of the first things Anders and Albert did after the rains returned and money became available was to buy new posts and re-fence all the pastures. Posts were placed every ten feet with new barbed wire. Albert sighted where each post was to go and was very proud of the straight fences that resulted from his hard work. The wooden yokes were put away because there were no more break-outs.

After the drought ended, the cattle were kept in a pasture—well supplied with water in a slough—a half-mile west of the barn. They had to be driven there in the morning along the road ditches, to drink the water there and then be brought home in the evening in time to be milked and watered at the well.

Whether the cattle were walking to the west pasture in the morning or returning to the barn in the late afternoon, they were always, during my childhood, led by the same cow—Beauty, a light roan with long horns, who tossed her head as she walked, as if to remind the rest of the herd that she was in charge. When they arrived at the water trough near the barn, she was the first to drink, standing at the trough undisturbed until she was satisfied. The rest of the cattle pushed and shoved one another as they drank, but none of them touched her. They all seemed to recognize her rank.

The Svendsbye siblings helped with a number of chores between the time they returned home from school and the supper hour. One of their tasks was to churn butter. The wooden churn and its stand were housed in the cellar and had to be carried up the stairs into the kitchen whenever they were used. The stand had a crank on it which the siblings often took turns rotating the churn around and around until the cream turned into butter. It was then taken out of the churn and salted before everything was washed and returned to the cellar. The butter that was churned on the farm was usually eaten there. The siblings also did the evening milking and cream separating before Anders and Albert returned from the field.

The family's evening meal—called supper—was served at 6:30, accompanied by two more fifteen-minute newscasts, one of which featured Morgan Beatty with his "News of the World" on the Mutual Broadcasting Company network. For the meal, there was always freshly baked bread and potatoes, generally boiled in their jackets. During the growing season, there were also usually vegetables from the garden, almost invariably peas or carrots, sometimes lettuce or radishes. In the winter there was fried fish. From time to time throughout the year, red meat was served in modest portions, used chiefly in stew or as pork chops or canned chunks of beef. Sometimes a chicken was butchered, one for the entire family, meaning that only one piece—a wing or a neck—might be available to each member. The family also liked cheese whenever it could be secured. Anders particularly liked a hard cheese called *gammelost*—which means "old cheese." Gudrun would put a chunk of it on a small plate and place it on the dining table in front of Anders. He would take out his pocketknife and—without washing it—carve off a piece of cheese, put it on his plate, and return his knife to his pocket.

Following the meal, there were chores in both the house and the barn. The dishes and the cream separator needed to be washed and dried. The horses and calves needed to be given water and hay. When those chores, and often others, had been completed, the time came to read—newspapers, magazines, or books. At 8:00 Anders turned on the radio to the Watrous, Saskatchewan, station to listen to the Canadian Broadcasting Company's "Summary of the Day's News." The remainder of the day provided a little more time to read and converse, until the family retired for the night, usually by 9:00 or 9:30. At that time every day, Anders wound the kitchen clock, set the alarm, and carried the clock into the bedroom. He also wound his one-dollar pocket watch, several of which he used during his lifetime. He never owned a wristwatch.

Anders butchered one hog late every fall after the temperature fell enough to freeze the meat in the unheated cook car. Gudrun canned as much of it as she could and put pork chops and other special cuts in a crock filled with lard, which preserved the meat without refrigeration. Following the custom in Norway, the blood was saved and used in certain foods. *Blodklubb* involved raw potatoes mixed in blood. Formed into balls about four inches in diameter, boiled, and served with butter, they were considered a special delicacy. During the winter, Anders bought a crate of fresh herring, also stored in the cook car. Gudrun would fry herring for the evening meal. Beginning about 1940, Wallace "Butch" Gjesvold installed electric freezer units—called lockers—in his butcher shop in Wildrose. They could be rented for storing meat. Anders did that, to the delight of the entire family.

Fruit was always welcome but not always on hand. At Christmas and on other rare occasions, Anders bought a crate of apples. Rarely did other fruit appear. Gudrun canned a few lugs—mostly pears and peaches—but they were generally reserved for guests who stopped by for short visits, for whom coffee, cookies, and a small dish of canned fruit would be served.

To stretch food, Gudrun created her own recipes. By adding bread crumbs to a can of salmon, she needed only one sixteen-ounce can to provide a decent-sized salmon patty for everyone at the table. Corn was never served as a vegetable. Normally, it would be prepared in heated skim milk and served as soup, which made it possible for a can of corn to feed a large family for one meal.

Nothing was wasted. There was little garbage. Leftovers were always eaten. Potato peelings were fed to the chickens or hogs. Most newspapers were burned in a stove for heat, as was most other paper. Pages from Sears and Montgomery Ward catalogs served as an essential item in the outhouse. Clothes were never given away. They were handed down to younger siblings, used as material to patch other clothing, or made into quilts.

Finding a place for everyone to sit and read with enough light at night was not easy. The reading area was the round dining table with a kerosene lamp in the center. In the early 1940s an Aladdin kerosene lamp, with a glowing mantle that produced much more light, was purchased. But if one needed space to write as well as read to do homework or if someone else wanted to spread out a newspaper or magazine, there was hardly space for more than four people at one time. Others had to retreat elsewhere. The problem was to find a place with enough light to see to read. There was no lamp in the downstairs bedroom, and the light from the kitchen lamp was dim. There was also the problem of finding a place to sit, because of the shortage of chairs.

And then there was the problem of finding enough places for people to sleep. When the number living at home was at its highest, a second bed was placed in the bedroom with Anders and Gudrun, with two beds in the living room. Bedsprings were bought and placed on boxes. Mattress covers were bought and filled with straw from the newest straw pile. The straw was replaced in the fall of each year.

There was little attention to play. On rare occasions, the children played cards, normally whist or hearts. There were few toys in the house. The girls had some dolls, the boys a few small metal horses and a couple of little rubber cars. Albert made a small barn out of apple boxes. We children pretended that empty spools from Gudrun's sewing machine were cattle. Those few items exercised our imaginations day after day as we scrambled across the linoleum-covered floors during the winter.

In warmer weather, Gudrun appreciated having the children play out in the farmyard. Imagination was equally important outdoors. We pretended we were farmers working in the fields. What else? Serving as horses were broken pitchfork handles or worn out pitmans—the wooden rods that linked the driving gear and moving sickles—discarded from the mower or binder. Worn out gears from farm machinery became fictional machinery that our imaginary horses pulled around the yard. Wire and binder twine held everything together. Some of us collected attractive stones or rocks in the fields. They became people, horses, or cattle as we found ways to enjoy ourselves without many manufactured toys.

Some of the usual teenage interests got little or no support from Anders and Gudrun. Dancing, smoking, and drinking alcohol were all prohibited. For the siblings, the most difficult prohibition was the one on dancing. Most teenagers in the area were allowed to dance, and that created its own kind of pressure. The young Svendsbyes all wanted to attend dances, and on rare occasions a couple of the girls did. To us it was both enjoyable and harmless. Smoking seemed harmless enough too, although expensive, so it was never a great temptation. Three of the sisters developed the habit later in life, but the rest of the siblings did not. Drinking beer had relatively little attraction.

While our parents' strictness inhibited certain youthful experiences, their openness to the future encouraged other things, including college education. Some of the older siblings had wanted to go to college but could not for want of money. There was not much more around as the younger children were finishing elementary school, but Anders and Gudrun encouraged plans to attend college. Nevertheless, when the question of going to Harvard or other Eastern schools was raised, the word came back: "We don't know how we'll get the money, but if that is what you want to do, you'll be able to." That was all the encouragement I needed. I attended college in Minnesota and did not go to an Eastern university until graduate school. But I never thought seriously about any other possibility after high school than going to college.[3]

Movies were not prohibited, although lack of money limited our ability to see many. To my knowledge, Anders and Gudrun saw only one. It was *One in a Million*, a 1936 Twentieth Century Fox film about Sonja Henie, Norway's world-famous Olympic skater. She won gold medals in women's Olympic figure skating at age fifteen in 1928 and again in 1932 and 1936. The first movie attended by the youngest children, including me, was a Shirley Temple film—I do not recall the title—in the late 1930s. Humphrey Bogart and Spencer Tracy were my favorite actors. *Thirty Seconds Over Tokyo*, featuring Spencer Tracy as Jimmy Doolittle, got my vote as the most memorable production.

There was always a dog, a male mongrel, on the farm. While they were special and treated with attentive care, they did not quite serve as companions, because they rarely accompanied anybody beyond the barnyard. Several generations of dogs resembled a collie, and all were named Rex. With one exception that comes to mind, they were never allowed in the house. During the winter, they were put in the hay shed at night, where they could curl up to sleep. Beginning in the spring, they remained outdoors, generally lying close to the north side of the house at night. Whenever it thundered, the dog headed for the barn and could usually be found hiding in a manger. None of the dogs were trained to herd cattle, but all of them were good watchdogs. The slightest disturbance in or near the farmyard was greeted with a bark and sometimes a growl. No strangers entered the yard without being scrutinized carefully.

The horses were all treated with great care and personal attention. Each had a name. When we stepped into their stalls, we frequently stopped to pat them and talk to them. Grooming them involved combing not only their hide but mane and tail as well. For water in the evening during the growing season, they were always led across a grassy knoll, where they would lie down to roll on the grass. When they got up, they shook themselves vigorously to get rid of the dust that had settled into their hide working in a field that day. Because they worked so hard in the fields, only a couple of the horses were ever used for horseback riding, and it was seldom that anyone rode them. All were regarded as work horses, and we held them in awe because of their strength and beauty. Those strong enough to pull the heaviest loads were held in especially high esteem.

We did not hunt. Anders had a shotgun, but he used it only to shoot animals before they were butchered. Albert did a fair amount of trapping, and he often snared jackrabbits. He set traps for other animals, such as weasels, when they appeared. He skinned the animals and took the furs to Wildrose or McGregor and sold them. In the 1930s, the skin of a jackrabbit sold for 10 cents.

One item that claimed the attention of everyone in the family was fuel. Obtaining fuel for heat and cooking was a problem from day one for everyone living on the treeless plains. Fortunately, coal was available nearby in large quantities. It was soft lignite coal that could often be located close to the earth's surface and excavated by strip mining. The closest lignite mines for the Svendsbye and Birkelo families were near Noonan, about twenty miles north. Coal mining, both surface and underground, became a major North Dakota industry later in the twentieth century.

Hauling the coal home was considered an adventure. Farmers would leave at 4:00 a.m. with a team of horses and a wagon box on wheels or on a sled, depending on the weather. They brought along generous quantities of sandwiches and coffee for the day's journey, as well as a sack of hay and some oats for the horses. They generally returned the same day, late at night, as the horses found their way in the moonlight across the prairie fields to a welcoming family. At times, coal was shipped in boxcars on the Great Northern to the Nelson Grain Elevator in Hamlet. Then farmers needed to come only a few miles to fill their wagon box or truck before heading home.

Because burning only coal was too expensive for some farmers, they found it necessary to supplement it with free alternatives. With few trees, wood was not a possibility, but dried manure would burn well. One task all the Svendsbye children had to perform was to take gunnysacks out into the pastures and fill them with dried cow and horse dung, bringing them home for Gudrun's use as she cooked and heated water to wash clothes.

Despite the hard work and somewhat primitive conditions under which they worked, Anders and Gudrun never expressed any regrets they might have had about leaving Norway, nor did they talk about Norway in any nostalgic way. Gudrun, of course, had no memories of life there, but she had a lively interest in Norway. Anders had spent the first twenty-two years of his life living and working there with his family. Yet only references to his sister's husband, Hans Andreas Moen, crept into any of Anders' conversations.

Hence when I went to Norway in 1955, my relatives were very much strangers to me. When I got to Drammen, I took a bus to Snarum where I was met by Uncle Ole's youngest daughter Marit. I have only the kindest memories of Ole and Marit, in part because they helped me communicate with the entire family despite my atrocious Norwegian. I would haltingly say a sentence, and one of them would re-state it, adding in Norwegian, "Is that what you meant to say?" Ole and his family were living on the Svendsby farm, and they invited me to be their guest. Never having had breakfast in bed before, imagine my surprise when Marit appeared at my bedside with a tray of delectable home-baked breads and other baked goods, only to discover that the real breakfast awaited me when I came downstairs. Ole did not own a car at that time, so he walked with me to the homes of both his sisters and his brother. Hans Andreas Moen lived up to his reputation by beginning our visit with Schnapps. When I said good-bye to Ole and his family, I told them that I would be back to visit them. "Yes," Ole said, "that is what they all say. But they don't do it." He was almost right about me. I did not return until the beginning of winter in 1991. Ole was dead. But Annelotte and I were greeted with incredible hospitality.

CHAPTER 7

Annual Rhythms

The Four Seasons

One of the beautiful things about life in North Dakota was that the climate, with frequent and dramatic contrasts, featured four distinct seasons of the year. Life was lived to exploit seasonal differences. Since nature's life emerged from under a snow cover in the spring, that season was the morning of a farming season that stretched from April—sometimes earlier—through September. The sun was the controlling force. It set the pattern for life on the North Dakota prairie. By the time the earth had rotated so that the sun's rays shone directly at the equator, it was melting the snow, watering and warming the soil so it could hospitably welcome the seeds that soon would be planted. The coming of spring was heralded by the birds and the prairie itself. The opening prelude came from the crow. It was not a favorite bird because of its destructiveness to other fowl of the air, but it was always gladly received when its loud call announced that winter was over and a new season was about to begin. Soon geese could be seen making their way back to Canada in beautiful formation. With the caw of the crows and the honk of the geese, the prairie sprang forth with new life. The grass grew green, and such few trees as there were sprouted buds that evolved into green leaves.

It all seemed like a grand celebration to a youngster on the land. Flowers soon adorned the prairie. First came purple crocuses, then bluebells, followed by marigolds and other flowers with differing colors. Ducks arrived and bobbed up and down on waves as they swam in the bright blue slough water, with the mallards attracting special attention because of their color. Soon meadowlarks were singing their beautiful melodies in fairly large numbers, joined by bluebirds and different kinds of blackbirds—red-winged, yellow-winged, white-winged—and a host of others, chirping and nesting. Barn swallows arrived shortly. We eagerly waited for the birds to build new nests or to reoccupy their old ones. Contrary to instructions, younger siblings would climb the trees to peek into the nests, count the eggs, and generally keep track of them until the baby birds were hatched. Not so with the nests of ducks or prairie chickens. Their nests were carefully hidden and were never disturbed in any way, lest the mother hens discover the intrusion and destroy them. We were always fascinated by the way prairie chickens tried to lead us away if we accidentally stumbled upon the place where the nest was hidden.

Anders was always one of the first in the community to welcome the spring and begin work in the fields. The first operation was to prepare the soil. He often began as early as the first week in April, which meant he had to wear gloves and a heavy jacket. Since he always farmed with horses, his machinery was simple—a plow or a disk. He had two plows. The smaller one, called a sulky plow, had only one moldboard and thus turned over the sod one twelve- or fourteen-inch row at a time. It was pulled by four horses and had an uncomfortable steel seat for the driver. The larger plow, called a gang plow, had two moldboards and turned over twice as much sod as the sulky in the same amount of time. It was pulled by five horses and had an equally uncomfortable seat. However, not all the land needed to be plowed. It could be disked, which was a four-horse operation designed to move around the topsoil and kill the weeds.

During the 1930s, when the land was terribly dry, thistles and other weeds grew densely. Sometimes the first operation on those acres was to remove the thistles by raking them in rows with a machine called a drag, then burning them. If the fields were unusually infected, Anders and later Albert would set fire to the entire field. Caution had to be used to keep the fires from spreading out of control. That was particularly hazardous because there were no fire trucks in the community. One had to use forks, shovels, and garden rakes to put out any flames that appeared at all threatening.

One spring Anders had an accident in the field that caused a "runaway." The four horses broke loose and ran. The harnesses had been hitched to an "evener," a six-foot piece of steel attached to the machine being pulled. For some reason, the piece connecting the evener to the plow broke, causing the evener to snap forward, hitting the horses on the backs of their legs. Startled, they leapt forward and broke away from Anders, leaving him stranded on the plow, the reins pulled from his hands. Eventually, the horses headed home, galloping at full speed, the evener trailing. Gudrun saw them coming and summoned Albert and me. We ran into the farmyard to catch them as they neared the house. To do so, one had to grab the reins dragging alongside the horses. That accomplished, we pulled on the reins until the horses, in obedience to the pull, began to run in circles and eventually slowed enough to make it possible to grab the bridle of the nearest horse. Once the horses stopped, they still were frightened and stood tensely, their heads held high and their ears pointed forward, snorting, ready to take off at the least provocation. None of the horses was hurt. Such accidents were rare, and this one did not interfere with the progress of the work season.

Having prepared the soil, Anders seeded the land with a ten-foot Van Burnt drill pulled by four horses. The drill prepared a furrow for the seed, sowed it, and covered it with soil. After the seed sprouted, some farmers sprayed their fields with a chemical to control the weeds. Anders did not like chemicals. "It is not good for the soil," he said. As a consequence, the yellow mustard weed grew and flowered with abandon in his fields, to the embarrassment of his sons.

Our farm was suited best for small grains: hard spring wheat, with some durum wheat, rye, flax, barley, and oats. The farm was too far north and the growing season too short for corn and soybeans. The soil was not rich enough for potatoes or sugar beets, high-producing crops in the Red River Valley along the North Dakota-Minnesota border. Seeding was generally completed in May or at latest during the first week in June.

The next operation was summer fallowing. During the 1930s, when the fields were dry, there was great wind erosion. To reduce erosion and improve the quality of the soil, the federal government encouraged farmers

Lloyd disking on a field in front of the house.

to divide their land into narrow strips and seed only half the land each year. The other half lay fallow and rested. In June that acreage was plowed and kept free of weeds the rest of the summer and fall by going over it several times with a disk. After the rains started, the plowed field could be muddy. One could always tell when the plowing was moist, because gulls swarmed across the field, picking up the worms from the newly-turned earth. The gulls formed a white-feathered escort for the horses as they moved back and forth across the field.

Strip farming, leaving half the land fallow each year, was one of the government's successful programs to combat the disasters of nature and of some earlier farming practices. In the 1930s those disasters included some incredible dust storms. Strong winds came out of the northwest and blew away the topsoil, filling the air with dust that was airborne for hundreds of miles. Sometimes, it was so thick it was difficult to see be-tween houses and barns. Some people tied a rope to their house and held onto it, so that when they reached their barn, they could find their way back to the house. Dust blew into houses with such force that floors and furniture were covered with a thin coating. Gudrun tried to prevent the dust from entering the house by stuffing rags around the inside windows, but it seeped in nevertheless. On windy days, she had to sweep and wash the floors and dust the furniture several times each day. One heard stories about some areas where the dust in the air was so thick that people chose not to sleep indoors. Instead, they would lie outside on the ground because the air was less polluted there when the dust blew overhead.

Little rain for several years meant there were few thunderstorms. They returned as the dry years faded. Dark blue clouds formed quickly, usually in the west, blotting out the sun. If really bad weather was on the way, vertical white lines appeared in the clouds. Those times, while not frequent, were eerie, especially at the moment the wind ceased after the dark clouds had formed and the air was completely still. When such times came in the evening, Anders went out into the yard to watch and study the cloud formations. He would return to the house once the rain started and the wind began to blow. On a couple of memorable occasions, when the wind was especially strong, he reentered the house and announced, "I think we had better go to the cellar." Out came a flashlight, up came the cellar door, and down the steps we went, to stand in the dark until the wind subsided. But most thunderstorms were fun rather than threatening, as we watched the brilliance of the lightning and listened to the thunder and the rain as it hit the house with force. When it was over, we emptied out of the house into the yard to look at the rainbow and to enjoy the fresh, cool air. While such storms were infrequent, they usually came in July at the end of the day, close to sunset.

July was the month for a new phase of summer work. It was haying, an operation tucked between summer fallowing and harvest. Preparation for haying began before the Fourth of July holiday. The mower needed to be oiled and greased, a more complex job than required of any other horse-drawn machine

Prince and Jack hitched to the mower in the farm yard.

except the binder. The gears were housed in the crankcase, which had to be opened and new oil poured in so that there was enough to bathe the moving gears in oil for the entire season. The sickles too had to be readied. Some were badly worn and had to be replaced; others had to be sharpened. Sharpening a sickle required the use of an emery wheel, about eighteen inches in diameter. The wheel was mounted on a steel frame and powered by pedals like those on a bicycle. To cut the hay quickly, each sickle bar had to be replaced by a newly sharpened one about every five hours. Haying itself usually began on the day after the Fourth of July. Anders almost always drove the mower himself. It was pulled by two horses.

The aroma of freshly cut hay was unmistakable. After drying, it was gathered into rows by a hay rake drawn by two horses. The hay had to be handled twice by men using four-tined pitchforks. First the hay was pitched from the rows into a hay-rack. It was pulled by a team of horses to a central place where the load was pitched onto a haystack. The work was strenuous and dirty. Albert, beginning in his early teens, did the stacking. He was proud of his straight, high stacks with perfectly rounded tops that kept rain from getting into the stacks and spoiling the hay.

Sometimes nature interrupted the work with showers that drenched both workers and the cut hay. In that case, nature also took care of the problem: It dried the hay in a day or two so work could proceed. If the hay had already been raked into piles, it was sometimes so wet that each pile had to be turned over by hand, one at a time. On a few occasions, the storm clouds gathered so quickly they exploded before one could exit from the hay field. When the clouds suggested hail was on its way, the horses were driven home at a fast clip in an attempt, sometimes in vain, to get both horses and humans under a roof before the hail pounded them.

Except in the dry years, there was always enough hay in the meadowland and in the sloughs and the ditches along the road to provide an adequate sup-

Haystack stacked by Albert in 1945.

ply, so Anders never seeded hay. The "meadowland" was forty acres of wild hay that Anders rented on the north edge of the Big Meadow. While only a mile and a half from home, that distance was considered too far to drive the horses home at noon while haying. Hence the noon meal was usually eaten in the shade of the hayrack, while the horses spent the entire noon hour eating hay. Gudrun tried to make the meals special, even though they were cold. The favorite fare was a hard-boiled egg with fresh bread and butter. As we lay under the hayrack resting after the meal, waiting for the horses to finish their lunch, we watched the differently shaped clusters of white clouds pass overhead. While we admired their beauty, we were more appreciative of their utility: cooling the earth as they passed.

While the men worked the fields, the coffee got cold and the drinking water got warm. Coffee was put in a half-gallon glass jar, which was wrapped in a dish towel and put in a gallon tin pail. It stayed warm for a time but not for long. The drinking water was put in a half-gallon tin pail that was put in the shade, if there was any. Especially on hot days, it got warm quickly. It was only after electricity was installed in 1949 that drinking water was chilled in the refrigerator, and it provided a cold drink on arrival home.

The weather drove the work of the farm forward. When the wheat and other grains ripened, harvest began. It started in the first half of August and continued late into September. The grain was cut and bundled using the binder. Invented by Cyrus McCormick in 1850 and first called a reaper, the device went through several evolutions before becoming the machine Anders used. It was pulled by four horses and always driven by Anders.

The four horses Anders most liked to drive were three lively grays—Nancy, Pat, and Daisy—and a large, brown-black gelding named Brigg. Nancy was the liveliest. When she stood in her stall in the barn, unless she was eating, she held her head high, with her ears moving back and forth to catch the slightest change in sound. When she was led out of the barn, she moved with high speed, which was also her speed in the field—with the result that she generally walked a foot or so ahead of her teammates, and with her head tossed several inches above her mates' heads. Daisy also walked quickly, especially if she was on the right. When turning left she ran, thus twirling the binder around as if on a high-speed chase. Anders preferred to drive her on the left, however, because she followed the grain so closely, with her head down, without requiring much attention from the driver. Pat kept pace with those two mates, but without their flair. Brigg was more of a plodder, but he took such big steps that he held his own, except when making the crucial left turn. All in all, the four moved the binder around the field with something approaching high speed.

Anders unloading bundles into the threshing machine in 1945.

The machine cut the grain, gathered it into bundles tied with twine, and dumped the bundles in rows to be gathered into shocks. Shocking was done by hand or by using a light three-tined fork. A shock was composed of six to eight bundles, carefully arranged to help the grain dry further and ripen completely. When Albert reached his teens, he did most of the shocking, although Gudrun sometimes helped. Earlier in her marriage she regularly worked in the fields to shock grain. Edward and I began assisting Albert when we were ten or eleven years old.

When the shocks were sufficiently dry, the final operation of harvest began—threshing. It usually started around Labor Day. Threshing involved a machine called a grain separator. Men, generally from the neighborhood, came with teams of horses pulling hayracks, which they drove along the rows of shocks as they pitched the bundles into the racks. When the load was full, they drove it alongside the separator. The bundles were pitched, heads first, into the mouth of the separator. The twine was cut by large knives, sending the heads of grain between rollers that separated the grain from the straw and chaff. The straw was blown out of the machine and formed a stack that was used to feed animals and provide clean bedding for animals in the barn. The grain poured from a spout and into a small bin next to the separator—or into wagon or truck boxes—then was hauled to the farmyard, where it was shoveled into grain bins. The grain was stored in those bins until it was shoveled into conveyances that took it to the elevator in Hamlet to be sold.

Harvest was regarded as fun but hard work. The fact that neighbors came together and assisted one another made the harvest more of a festive social affair than was the case with most other farming operations. During threshing everybody ate better. Breakfast included bacon, pancakes, waffles, or French toast. Meat was served at both dinner and supper: roast beef, pork roast, pork chops, meatballs, ham, or chicken, together with potatoes, gravy, and vegetables. There was always fresh bread and pie. Threshers came to know which farms in the community served the best meals—a fact that encouraged perennial competition among cooks.

The men slept in the haymow at each farm where they threshed. Each carried a bedroll—a blanket or two tied to the back of their hayrack. They were spread out in the haymow. Taking off only their shoes, they crawled between the blankets and slept until five in the morning. After feeding, combing, and harnessing the horses, they went to the house, where a couple of basins on boxes and a pail of warm water were waiting outside for them to wash their hands and faces. Inside, as they all sat around a table eating, they visited and told stories and jokes before leaving for the barn to hitch up their horses and get quickly to the field to be ready to unload the first bundle load at seven. There was a celebrative air about the entire enterprise.

Anders allowed me to drive a solid, gentle team of bays—six-year-old Rowdy and eight-year-old Prince. Prince was one of the two gentlest horses Anders owned at the time. The two horses stood together in the barn. Prince rarely moved. Rowdy was somewhat restless. When the time came for the horses to be fed oats, Rowdy neighed and pawed the ground in front of his manger, while Prince waited motionlessly. Out in

The Nelson Grain Company in Hamlet as it is today. The lower wooden structure on the right is a remodeling of the original elevator built in 1910.

the harvest fields, the pair followed the rows of shocks perfectly, rarely requiring a signal to move a bit closer to or farther from the row. One gave them a one-sound signal to start or stop. Rowdy's left front leg was slightly enlarged, so he walked with a faint limp. When the team ran, for the sake of that leg he preferred to lope rather than run. Both horses loved to be patted and to have their necks scratched.

Harvest was also a time to make money. Albert and I were not paid for shocking at home, but we were paid 75 cents to a dollar an hour for shocking for our Olson neighbors. For the work of the threshing machine, the owner was paid according to the number of bushels harvested. He in turn paid the rest of the workers. Bundle haulers got 90 cents to a dollar an hour, with an additional 10 cents per hour for each of the two horses. The money earned each year from threshing was sufficient to pay for my clothes, school supplies, and spending money.

Fall Days and Celebrations

After threshing, a few other essential operations remained before winter's arrival. One of the most important was digging potatoes. The previous spring the sulky plow was pulled across the plot set aside for growing potatoes, and parts of a potato, each cut to contain one eye, were planted a few inches apart in the furrow made by the plow. As the potato plants grew, each row had to be cultivated to get rid of the weeds. Sometimes red bugs would come, seemingly out of nowhere, to infect the plant. Since we did not spray and because the bugs often clung to the underside of the leaves, the bugs had to be picked from the plants by hand and destroyed to prevent them from damaging the plants by eating their leaves. This task was performed by the younger siblings.

Each plant produced several potatoes. To extract them from the ground when they had grown to an appropriate size, the plow again was used to turn over the soil row by row, leaving the potatoes on top of the earth to be picked by eager hands and stored in the cellar for later use. If other vegetables were still growing in the garden, they too needed to be picked or dug for storage at this time.

The summer fallow had by now grown weeds, which needed to be removed by disking. Coal had to be bought and stored. After the cold weather arrived, a hog was butchered.

One of the less attractive tasks was putting manure from the barn around the entire house, about three feet high and two feet thick, to help keep the house warm. Whenever outdoor temperatures fell much below zero at night, Gudrun had to remove all the jars of canned goods from the cellar. After she and Anders had finished their bedtime coffee, she took a pan downstairs, gathered jars of canned fruit and meat, carried them up into the living room, and put them on the dining table, making as many trips as were necessary. In the morning, before breakfast, she returned them to the cellar—until the next extra-cold night, when she would repeat the process. Putting manure around the house ended in 1944 when the house, left unpainted for decades, was painted a gleaming white.

Handling manure, long done annually for the house, was a daily task in the barn. During the summer, there were only the horses and calves to be taken care of there, but during the winter, with the cattle in the barn also, the task was larger. Each day, the manure had to be put in a short wagon box or a manure spreader, to be hauled to the manure pile or spread on the fields. Anders and a neighbor had bought a manure spreader after World War I, but it remained at the neighbor's farm most of the time. That meant that both the loading and unloading of the manure was done by hand with a four-tine fork.

One major problem on the Svendsbye farm, requiring all sorts of work, was providing water for both humans and animals. Anders had dug at least three shallow wells, each between fifteen and twenty feet deep.

Two were situated near a slough, not far from the barn. While those two wells lasted, the horses and cattle were led or chased to the wells. The water was put in metal tubs that could be carried from one well to the other—necessary because as the wells began to go dry, only enough water seeped into each to fill a tub or two a couple times a day. Water for the calves was carried in buckets from the wells into the barn. Eventually, the shallow wells went dry. Other farmers dug wells not much deeper than Anders' and struck a water vein that kept them supplied year-round throughout the dry years. Anders was not so fortunate.

Water for the animals was always plentiful in the sloughs during the spring, after the runoff from the melting snow was collected. But when the sloughs dried up, water had to be hauled from the neighbors. About six wooden or steel barrels were put in a low wagon box and hauled on a wagon or sled by a team of horses every other day. Albert was generally responsible for that task. During the winter, the barrels had to be stored in the barn so that the water did not freeze.

Water for humans was always hard to come by. Drinking water and water used for cooking was hauled from various places in five-gallon cans that had been initially used for shipping cream to the creamery by rail. Almost every time Anders drove to Hamlet or McGregor he took along a cream can so that he could fill it at the village well and bring the water home for storage in an eight-gallon crock in the cellar and a similar vessel standing in the kitchen.

Water for washing clothes was a different matter. In the warm months, rain that ran off the roof of the house was saved in barrels. Barrels of water were also hauled from sloughs or ditches as needed. In the winter, many tubs of snow were taken from snow banks in the farmyard and melted in tubs sitting on the top of the cook stove in the kitchen. Because of its scarcity, water had to be conserved and, where possible, reused. Siblings took their weekly baths upstairs in a tub. Usually several bathed in the same water.

In 1941, after the first good crop following the drought and Depression, Anders hired a man to drill a 135-foot-deep well. That solved the problem of watering the animals, but the water had too many minerals to be used for human consumption, and the minerals spotted clothes, so could not be used for laundry. But the well solved the major water problem on the farm by providing water for the animals. At first the water—as much as 200 gallons—was pumped by hand. On cold winter days, with a strong wind coming from the northwest and before a well house finally arrived, one's face got very cold while pumping the amount of water the animals required—and sometimes the face froze. When that happened, snow was held against the frozen area to help bring blood circulation back to the tissue so it could thaw without damage. After about a year, Albert bought a gasoline engine

The well and the pump engine in the winter of 1942-43.

to do the pumping. When the federal government's Rural Electrification Administration (REA) brought electricity to the farm following World War II, an electric motor was purchased to power the pump, and a few years later an old granary was moved into place to serve as a well house. It was as though a new world had opened.

About every ten years after the first deep well was brought in, enough sand had filtered in to plug it, and a new and deeper one was dug. In the 1960s, a third deep well was required. By that time, Anders and Gudrun had moved to Tioga, and Albert had brought in a large trailer house in which to live. Now devices were available to remove impurities from the water and to make it drinkable. Pressure pumps were installed. After six decades, running water was available for both house and barn, for both animals and humans, with the turn of a faucet.

The frequency with which drinking water had to be hauled to the farm from a well just outside Hamlet had two positive consequences during the summertime. Most important, the mail was brought home regularly from the Hamlet Post Office so that newspapers could be read while the news was still fresh. In addition, during World War II, as better crops were being harvested and there was a bit more cash on hand, Anders or Albert would sometimes buy a pint of ice cream—the smallest quantity available—which had to be eaten immediately because there was no freezer. Each person got a thin slice—less than one scoop—but it was enough for the memory to last a lifetime. No treat was as enjoyable, except possibly the rare purchase of a few bananas.

Freezers did not arrive on the Svendsbye farm until after World War II. When the REA brought electricity to nearly all farmsteads in western

North Dakota in 1949, significant changes occurred. Electric lights in the house made it seem almost palatial. Soon Gudrun acquired a refrigerator, an electric washing machine, a small electric stove, and an electric iron. There was never air conditioning, but the new electric stove meant the kitchen stayed much cooler in summer. With the refrigerator, the drinking water was always cold, and ice cream was always on hand. The battery radio was replaced with an electric one, and soon there was a television set to bring the world into the living room. Lights were installed in the barn. Outdoors, powerful yard lights went up on all the farms in the community, flooding the farmsteads with light, dotting the dark prairie nights, and announcing to the world that another benefit of city living had come to the country.

Considering the large number of people in the family, illnesses were rare. Anders was seldom sick, but when he was, Dr. Goodman from Powers Lake was called to the farm. Shortly before World War II, Anders became ill with a severe cough. After Dr. Goodman had examined him and diagnosed pneumonia, Anders asked him what could be done about it. Anders was a heavy smoker who smoked both pipes and hand-rolled cigarettes. He carried his tobacco cans in a chest pocket of his overalls. Goodman eyed the pipes, cigarette paper, and tobacco lying nearby, then asked directly, in his customary fashion, "Do you want to live?"

Anders was caught off guard by the question but responded, "Of course."

"Well," Goodman replied, "if that's the case, then you had better throw away your tobacco." Anders quit cold turkey and never smoked again. Goodman was perhaps the only doctor and maybe the only human being who could have pulled that off, because Anders trusted him explicitly, even about the effects of tobacco, long before that matter gained national attention.

Gudrun had at least three surgeries at the Good Samaritan Hospital in Williston. She had back pain, sometimes severe, but it was never diagnosed or treated, except with an occasional aspirin. Alice, second oldest of the children, was the only one who might have been called unwell. She had rheumatic fever as a child. As a result, she had a weak heart and had to be careful not to overexert herself. There were also the more common childhood diseases, like measles and mumps, as well as the removal of tonsils and adenoids. But on the whole, the family seems to have been quite healthy.

One of the highlights the children enjoyed as they grew to adulthood was a car trip to Williston, about fifty miles away. Such a trip was not

A lonely picture of North Dakota.

taken unless it was necessary. Because Williston was the county seat, Anders needed to go there from time to time to conduct business for the farm and for boards on which he served. He served on a Williams County committee for the Federal Land Bank, which met periodically. That and other business provided opportunities for Gudrun and one or two of the siblings to accompany him. It was a major event. During the winter, bricks were heated and placed on the floor of the back seat to keep feet warm, because there was no heater in the car. While in Williston, Gudrun shopped primarily at J. C. Penney and Woolworth's, because items there were the most affordable. Penney's had opened its first store in North Dakota in 1912 and by 1935 had thirty-three in the state.[1] The noon meal was usually eaten at the Luzon Café where Anders, after thoughtfully surveying the menu, always ordered halibut. The courthouse provided a genuinely humane service to all city visitors by having large public restrooms in its basement. Before returning home, Gudrun normally stopped at a bakery to buy a few cinnamon rolls to give all the children a chance to participate in the day's adventure when she and Anders returned home. That simple pleasure was so anticipated that, as a child, if I had remained at home, I would stand at the west window of the living room to watch eagerly for the family car to appear over the hill in anticipation of such a grand treat as a frosted cinnamon roll.

Other celebrative events included the many birthdays in a family of ten children. Most often there were no gifts, but there was always a cake.

Occasionally, the Birkelos or other neighbors came by to sample the cake and drink some coffee while everyone visited. Holidays provided the best opportunity for family celebrations, including special opportunities for visitation among the neighbors. As casual visits were fairly frequent during other times of the year, Thanksgiving, Christmas, New Year's, and sometimes Easter were more elaborate occasions. A group of neighbors exchanged invitations for dinner on those winter holidays. The adults enjoyed the visits, but the children were interested mainly in the meals. For the adults and some of the older children, there was always lutefisk. The younger children had different tastes and were accommodated with meatballs, roast beef, or roast pork. Of course, there were also mashed potatoes and gravy, as well as vegetables and a variety of other homemade foods such as flatbread and different kinds of pickles. But topping the list was lefse and different varieties of pie.

While the grandparents lived, the Birkelos were active participants in the family dinner exchanges. After Margaret and Gilmer Vatne married, the rest of the Vatne family was always included. Anders and Gudrun and Gilmer's parents, Knut and Caroline, became good friends. Both women were excellent cooks.

Who could forget the dining table Caroline prepared? It was laden with all kinds of delicious food. Yet when inviting people to the table, she would say in typical Norwegian fashion, "We haven't got much, but help yourselves to what we have." At one Christmas dinner in the midst of the Depression, Knut was heard saying, "A person can't really complain when there is lutefisk like this!" He had a heavy mustache that carried its own fascination for a curious child who watched the eating process carefully. How could he drink his coffee without getting his mustache wet?

Sitting in the Vatne living room, one could look up and see a picture of a somber man wearing an odd hat. Told that he was Martin Luther but seeing no connection to the Lutheran church, one wondered, "Why do they have his picture hanging there?"

Gudrun made Christmas festive not only with the special foods she prepared but also by decorating our home with red paper bells and streamers of red crepe paper. For a few years during the Depression there were no Christmas trees nor Christmas gifts. Beginning in 1938, a small Christmas tree with candles reappeared and inexpensive gifts were given. There was only one gift per person, usually something one could wear, plus apples and a small quantity of candy and nuts. That was deemed adequate by all.

Easter was also observed in a special way, although it was not as festive as Christmas. The Christmas snow had been replaced with the Easter mud, but a worship service was scheduled at Grong during the week prior to Easter if the weather and the roads allowed it. Gudrun often made a particularly tasty bread for Easter Sunday breakfast, which was served with a rare appearance of hard-boiled eggs. There were also Easter visits with neighbors from time to time, but only for afternoon coffee rather than for a main meal.

There were special Memorial Day ceremonies at the Wildrose School. The program included patriotic songs and the recitation of "In Flanders Fields." A guest speaker and the presentation of flags by the American Legion was also standard. The cemeteries in the entire community were decorated. Led by Gudrun, the Svendsbye family went to Grong cemetery on the day prior to Memorial Day to weed the family graves as well as the graves of persons whose families no longer lived in the community, and to place artificial flowers on each grave. Artificial flowers were used because they lasted longer and did not require watering.

On the Fourth of July, celebrations were held only in the larger towns which Anders deemed were too far away to attend. So we celebrated privately. Sometimes that involved a family picnic. There was always a special meal with a special dessert. That meant a pie, which most often was apple or lemon. Small firecrackers, maybe ten of them, were purchased. Everyone at home gathered at dusk to watch them explode. Our neighbors to the east, Christ Olsons, had a more elaborate collection of firecrackers so we always watched their fireworks as a part of our holiday.

Labor Day was observed in near silence. It was a silence as sacred as any memory recalls. This was the working man's holiday. We were proud to be a part of the blue collar group. Commitment to that day as rest was never broken as best my memory can recall. The threshing season started the day after Labor Day. If neighbors were seen to be doing anything more than required chores for the lives of animals, Albert greeted their activity with an extensive oath.

Minor holidays, like Valentine's Day and Halloween, were noted but not celebrated. We bought a few inexpensive valentines, ordered from the Sears Roebuck or Montgomery Ward catalogue, but they were not given to other members of the family, only to school friends. Thus only six holidays were observed with special emphases: Easter, Memorial Day, the Fourth of July, Labor Day, Thanksgiving Day, and Christmas. They were essentially all holy days, during which outdoor work was limited to watering and feeding the animals and milking the cows. Sundays were also observed as days of rest except during the harvest season.

But of all the holidays, Christmas was the celebration that superseded all others in its impact. It was a joyous occasion. The songs—both sacred and secular—the tree, the foods, the home decorations, the gifts, the programs, and the visits produced great moments that are extraordinarily memorable.

Some of the events on the prairie a child remembered were not human at all, even though they were a part of the human experience. Some were cosmic events in which people could only be spectators, especially the dramatic North Dakota sunrises and sunsets, the latter closely followed by the stars lighting up the entire night sky, with the majestic Big Dipper shining down most brightly. North Dakotans found that awesome.

Other weather events will never be forgotten by those who experienced them. The melancholy winds were often so strong they made bodily movement nearly impossible. The dust storms, rainstorms, hailstorms, snowstorms, and tornadoes were equally memorable. Like Pearl Harbor or the terrorist attacks of September 2001, some storms are, for those who experienced them, dates in history. Such was the tornado of June 18, 1919, that killed a neighbor and shot two-by-fours straight through his house. There was the tumultuous rainstorm of 1935 that caused what little crop there was to lodge and thus rust on the vine. In the summer of 1942 came the hailstorm that nearly wiped out a good crop for neighbors just north of Hamlet. And in 1943 a March snowstorm blocked roads and halted all traffic, forcing school closings for nearly a week.

As one thinks of all nature's varied beauty on the North Dakota prairies, spring time outshone them all. Life emerging from under the snow, covering the entire prairie with a bright green decorated with a few colorful flowers, serenaded by the meadow larks and the mallards, was—as the current expression has it—awesome.

CHAPTER 8

Changes

After World War II, the United States changed. Even the weather changed. The rains which had returned to the prairie a few years earlier continued, and prospects for farming looked good. In spite of this, people continued to leave. I was a high school student by this time, and I wondered why our neighbors were quitting and moving away, most often it seemed to the west. At such times, a public auction was held. My interest in them ran so high that my father allowed me to miss school to attend local auctions—which also happened to be where he bought most of his horses. For me, the excitement of the auction was commingled with questions as to why these farmers were quitting even as good times were returning. Such questions were never really answered.

By this time Anders Svendsbye had become a prominent leader on the local scene. Except for a three-year period, he had served on the Big Meadow Township Board from 1932 to 1957 and the Hamlet School Board for nearly as long, beginning in 1926, sometimes as chairman of both boards. One of his township board duties, which thoroughly delighted all the family, was to co-sign all the warrants issued by the township. The signing ceremony provided an evening of merriment that the family long remembered. Christ Olson, our closest neighbor, was the township clerk who regularly brought a batch of warrants over for Anders' signature. Christ was the best storyteller in the neighborhood and kept the entire family rollicking all evening as he embellished accounts of what was happening in the community.

In addition to serving on the township and school boards, Anders was equally proud to be chosen as a member of the Williston National Farm Loan Association. It advised the Federal Land Bank officer in Williston—who was secretary-treasurer of the association—what action he should take with respect to loan applications from farmers in the area. He was proud of this service and quietly satisfied with it. His family, his farm, and community leadership were the three activities or priorities he integrated into his life to give it purpose and meaning.

He was disappointed when the population in the area decreased to the point where he had to lead in closing the high school, which had been the flower of community pride for two decades. But with almost no students and, consequently, a shortage in funding, there was no choice. The decision to close having been made, however, the family confronted a new question: Where would the Svendsbye children now go to school? Given the interest in that question by the entire family, one might envision one or more family discussions about the matter. But there were none, except perhaps privately between Anders and Gudrun. In conformity with the usual family protocol, there was only an announcement. The children were simply told: They would all transfer to McGregor.

But McGregor was new territory, six miles away! Most of the Svendsbye siblings had barely visited the town. Wildrose and Williston were more familiar. Nevertheless, in the fall of 1943, the Svendsbye children were transferred to McGregor. It was a significant shift for the entire family—like moving to a new community. But it turned out to be a good decision, one that was repeatedly celebrated with thanksgiving. All the siblings were welcomed to the school, which quickly became as important, and then even more important, than the school in Hamlet.

During our first year at McGregor, there were two teachers for the high school and three for the elementary grades. The two high school teachers, Evelyn Johnson and Florence Borstad, were outstanding. Miss Johnson taught a course in "civics" or "citizenship" that included her emphasis on understanding the national and state constitutions. She described the U.S. and North Dakota constitutions and the responsibilities and opportunities of citizenship in an engaging manner, without preaching. Miss Borstad taught English grammar with insight and effectiveness that for most of us was probably never replicated. She made diagramming sentences understandable, even enjoyable. During our junior and senior years, Eileen Lofgren and Gloria Loe also proved to be outstanding English teachers. Because there were only two high school teachers, no electives were offered, but the breadth of the curriculum was enough to satisfy most curiosities and provided a solid preparation for college, especially if one were interested in the humanities.

One of the important contributions the McGregor School brought to its students was the library. The holdings were few but well chosen. The school also made use of the state's lending library. The school and any interested student had available—within a few days or weeks—almost any good current or classic novel, biographies of persons from politicians and poets to physicians and scientists, as well as books about the geography, life, and cultures of nations the world over. Already in my life, biographies claimed my attention more frequently than novels. One of the most valuable books available for use in the classroom or assembly hall was the *World Almanac*. It had data about almost everything of interest. Almost as interesting was the *North Dakota Blue Book*, an almanac of the state—still published—that reported on legislative sessions, the weather, grain prices, and other significant events in the state. Both books challenged the development of memorization skills to help one retain important data about the world.

Books in the school library or from the state lending library often stimulated discussions among students during free time. Helen Clapesattle's biography of the Mayo brothers led to lengthy discussions about the wonder and difficulty of the medical profession. Political biographies stirred equally lively discussions, especially any concerning the New Deal because of Roosevelt's use of federal funds on behalf of the needy. There was about equal support for both sides. I don't recall that we read any books with religious themes. We did, however, have passionate discussions about community practices and opinions that frowned on intermarriage between Catholics and Protestants and between Christians and Jews. Such attitudes were regarded by most students as narrow-minded. Almost as a testimony to our assumed broadmindedness, we chose as the speaker for our graduation a woman lawyer from Powers Lake whom we wanted to call to the community's attention.

There were only a few extracurricular activities. There was basketball for the boys. A two- or three-act play was presented annually. Occasionally a small group made an effort to form a chorus. A herculean effort was made to publish an annual and sometimes a newspaper. There was no band until the late 1950s. The social high point of the year was a fall school carnival with various booths and activities, for which tickets were sold. It funded a trip to some place of interest to the senior class. For the class of 1947 it was a trip to the Black Hills in South Dakota.

High school basketball had an exciting history of high achievement in both Hamlet and McGregor, but not while I participated. Perhaps that was because there was little discipline about practicing and learning plays. Sometimes there was no coach. During World War II gasoline was rationed, restricting the use of cars to transport the team for practice or games. Sometimes the entire team sat in the back of a pickup covered with a tarp as we moved from town to town. A few times we traveled by train.

As had been the case at Hamlet, Anders and a neighbor agreed to drive their children to and from school in alternate weeks. The daily trips were usually uneventful, but occasionally classes were canceled because of snow. One snowstorm came suddenly in the middle of the day, and we almost did not get home. The snow was falling so fast and the wind was blowing so strongly that it was impossible to see more than a few feet ahead of the car. At one point, Albert walked in front of the car to help Anders stay on the road.

The school seems to have been much more effective than the church in shaping young lives. To be sure, the school had a significant time advantage over the church. It had hundreds of hours at its disposal each year, in contrast to only dozens of hours annually available to the church. Both were concerned about the acquisition of knowledge, but the school used its time to develop knowledge with understanding. It invited student participation in the educational process through discussion and questioning, which in turn fostered inquisitiveness and stimulated the imagination. The church, on the other hand, used its time to transmit knowledge by emphasizing memorization and indoctrination, without questions, without discussion. That stifled inquiry, minimized understanding, and reduced interest. Moreover, the church seems to have focused mainly on life after death, while the school looked squarely at the here and now, which was of greater interest, especially to the young.

The difference in approach can be illustrated by the generous use of literature by the school and its limited use by the church. The school made available a wealth of books and a few magazines, all designed to help the student better learn and understand the subject under scrutiny. The church lifted up only two books: the Bible and Martin Luther's Small Catechism, without any other literature that might have helped the confirmands understand those primary texts.

In one area while I was a teenager, church and school were about equal participants as they functioned as centers for community social activity. The church sponsored choral concerts at Christmas and Easter. Young people's programs—presentations by church members of school age consisting of songs by a variety of small groups as well as recitations and readings—were scheduled as often as once a month following worship. The school, on the other hand, sponsored basketball games, musical concerts, declamation contests, and a few dances and carnivals. Attendance at those events was usually limited to the Hamlet community.

A different sort of activity was "cash night." During summer months in the 1940s, the Wildrose merchants sponsored a weekly outdoor amateur evening. Musical instruments were played, popular songs were sung as solos or by ensembles, and other entertainment acts were performed. As an added attraction, names were drawn from a hat for the winners of three small cash prizes. Community interest and excitement was always high. The entire Svendsbye family attended.

In the midst of all this change, farmers prospered. Politics, which fueled the farm lobby both inside and outside Congress, kept a pretty steady floor on farm prices. Federal farm programs, as well as domestic and eventually foreign markets, stimulated and undergirded the agricultural industry. This enabled farmers to not only plan in ways that could help avert economic disasters of the kind that had plagued the prairie for decades, but also to make farm life more secure.

Signs of growing prosperity also left its mark on the community. New and remodeled houses popped up on farms and in the small towns that characterized the prairie. Upgraded gas and electrical appliances became commonplace. New implement and grain storage facilities, as well as new trucks, pickups, cars, and other modern farm machinery appeared in rapid succession. Television arrived in many farm homes.

But expansion and mechanization of the Svendsbye farm was at a standstill. Some years earlier, Anders had made one of the most critical decisions of his life. If farm income would someday increase, he would give priority to paying his debts rather than investing in the expansion of his farm. A tractor and other new machinery would have to wait. Even buying more land at a time when prices were dirt cheap was postponed until it was too late as all the land was bought up by others. Anders' farm thus continued to be powered by horses and human muscle and remained labor-intensive so long as he was in charge. Why? Debt and age. Regardless of what others wanted or thought, Anders had made up his mind. He wanted to pay all his debt before he died. Until that was done, there was no money for anything else. And with each passing year, he came closer to the time when age would require him to step aside.

Age was the driving factor. The transition occurred in the early 1950s. Most of the debt was paid when Anders became seventy years of age in 1952. Other problems confronted him. The horses too were getting old and needed to be replaced, but Albert opposed buying more of them. So in 1949, Albert bought a used International 10-20 tractor from a neighbor. Anders now saw that he had come to the end of an era. Three years later, he used some of his mineral acres to buy an International W-6 tractor. It was the only motorized machine he ever purchased for the

Albert with his chisel plow and International tractor parked in front of his house on the farm.

farm, except for two steam engines he used for threshing. Area machinery dealers were exchanging new tractors for mineral acres, which had become valuable a year earlier when oil was discovered near Tioga. While Anders bought the tractor, he never drove it. Younger people could do that.

As years went by, Albert bought larger and more powerful machines. Operations to prepare the soil—plowing and disking—were the first to be powered by a tractor's internal combustion engine rather than horses. Next was the drill to seed grain. The last major function to be fully mechanized was the entire harvest operation. In 1954, a half-century after Anders arrived to select his homestead, Albert purchased a swather to cut the grain and began hiring combines and their crews to thresh it.

The generational change began in earnest. Albert did not just take over the farm, he also assumed responsibility for taking care of his aging parents. Anders and Gudrun had no savings and only a modest income from Social Security. Albert solved their problem by doing three things: he did the farming; he paid for all the new machinery and fuel to operate them; and he insisted that the income from the farm go to Anders and Gudrun. They now had a source of income for the rest of their lives. Albert financed all that with his earnings from working full time in the Tioga oil fields and from income from a quarter section of land he rented. He did not have the sole responsibility to do what he did—there were nine other children in the family. But he chose to do it that way, and his will prevailed. That was one of the ways families took care of the older generation before the responsibility was largely absorbed by government.

Vatnes combining in the 1980s.

A few years later, Albert took over the farm entirely. Anders became ill and stepped aside completely. He even gave up driving the last car he owned, a 1952 Chevrolet purchased in 1955. Meanwhile, time moved quickly.

Some of Albert's Herford cattle in the late 1980s.

Most of the Svendsbye children left home, one at a time. The two oldest sisters left home to marry. Albert remained at home. So did Edward, for a time. The others left to attend more school. Lillian went to nursing school, and Gladys and Ida to business college. Lloyd, Adeline, and Jean all chose the same liberal arts college: Concordia in Moorhead. Those six all married and settled in various parts of the United States. Albert and Edward served in the U.S. Army—Albert in Japan, Edward in Germany. I lived in Germany as a student. These international experiences, in different ways, shaped what we thought about life and our country's role in the world.

After a half-century of tumultuous activity involving two world wars, a Depression that affected the entire globe, and a drought that drove a majority of the immigrants off the land, Anders and Gudrun soon saw themselves nearing the end of their eventful lives. The old farmhouse became too

The Svendsbye house in the mid-1940s.

The Svendsbye family picture taken in 1946.

cold for them to live in during the winter, so they found and moved into a warmer place in McGregor. It was near enough to the public school for Jean to walk there. After she graduated from high school, they wintered in Tioga. In 1964 they moved permanently to Tioga, where their Dakota journey really had begun at the train station almost sixty years earlier. For the first time in their lives, they had both electricity and running water.

By this time Anders was bedridden and needed constant care from Gudrun. Anders did not want to go into a nursing home. He and Gudrun both believed strongly that a family should take care of itself and not depend on others for support. So for the closing years of their lives Gudrun provided Anders with nursing care twenty-four hours a day. She fed him, engaged him in conversation, and regularly gave him back rubs. She changed and washed his sheets several times a day—grateful for running water and an electric washing machine. Several times a day she tenderly lifted him to move him. Without her cheerful and meticulous care, Anders could never have lived as long as he did.

Throughout their marriage, they were supportive of each other through thick and thin. In many respects they were opposites. Anders had more settled opinions than Gudrun. He was more direct and assertive. A good conversationalist, he almost never talked about Norway or about himself. He rarely laughed, except when listening to what he considered a funny story. At times he was moody. When something went wrong, he could get excited and angry and sometimes swore in Norwegian.

Once when I was sixteen, Anders, as was his custom, was working on the binder to get it ready for harvest. Something went wrong and he became very angry, cursing in Norwegian. I said to him, "Dad, why do you have to get so angry?"

He turned and said to me, "Are you going to leave me?" I did not know what to do or say, so I put my arms around him and hugged him as tightly as I could. He burst into tears and sobbed.

Gudrun was more winsome, low-key, and even-tempered. She enjoyed talking with her family or anyone else who might have been present. She delighted in telling her children stories about her childhood and had a strong sense of caring for people—neighbors and family. She worked faithfully as a member of Grong Ladies Aid, the principal social organization for women in the community. She did not want to be an officer, but she always reported for duty when the church needed to be cleaned, when dinners were being served, or when someone was needed to wash the dishes. She also spent many hours sewing and crocheting items for sale at the Ladies Aid annual auction.

Anders and Gudrun agreed on all central matters. Anders insisted upon being informed about what was happening in the world. He subscribed to several newspapers almost the entire time he lived on the prairie. Later he listened regularly to newscasts on the radio, although he rarely watched television. Gudrun was not as interested in public affairs. She did, however, pay close attention to both radio and television newscasts. Neither was inclined to be critical of neighbors or of their community. On the contrary, they were proud of their community and celebrated their neighbors' achievements. Both distanced themselves from any actions they deemed objectionable, but were cordial to all.

They disagreed about some political issues, but they never let such matters divide them from each other or from their neighbors. They embraced Republicans and Democrats in their friendship circles. What they objected to and disliked was pretension in any form. Both had a strong sense of equality and could be offended by acts deemed pompous. They were alert to what transpired in the several communities of which they were a part and were respectful of their neighbors, however differently they might think or act. Whatever criticisms they had of others—with the exception of public-office holders—they kept to themselves or at least within their family.

What they said to their children they considered a private matter. Their offspring were scolded and praised evenhandedly. They governed their children while they were at home. But when the children left home, Anders and Gudrun granted them complete freedom. If any of their children wrote asking for advice, their response was always some version of "It is your life. You decide."

They died contentedly with their children all honorably launched on lives of their own. That was their chief satisfaction. Anders died first, after a lingering illness. He died in the Tioga Hospital, at age eighty-five, on May 30, 1967. His funeral was at Grong Church in Hamlet on June 2. It was the last funeral at the church, which was closed after the Sunday service the following day and torn down three years later. Following the service, thirteen neighbors

Gudrun and Anders Svendsbye with Jean and Albert, 1958.

who were all honorary pallbearers, formed two rows outside the church entrance and stood at attention. Between those rows, members of the family walked and carried Anders' casket from the church to the waiting hearse. He was buried in Grong Cemetery, one and one-half miles east from where he had lived for more than half a century.

After Anders' death, Gudrun planned something she had always wanted to do: visit each of her children in their homes scattered around the United States. But first she was going to have surgery in the Tioga hospital. There she died of a heart attack on March 8, 1968, at age sixty-six. Her funeral was on March 13 at Grace Lutheran Church in Wildrose, where she had been confirmed. She was buried beside her husband in Grong Cemetery, under the prairie soil.

When I visited Anders for the last time, I asked him what items or events in his life he was most proud of. Quickly, while lying in bed, he raised the upper part of his body with his right arm, looked straight at me, and said, "I paid all my debts."

Endnotes

Chapter 1

1   For administrative purposes, Norway is divided into nineteen districts called *fylker*. Each *fylke* is subdivided into smaller units called *kommuner*. A *fylke* is generally the size of several counties in the United States. A *kommuner* is generally the size of several U.S. townships.

2   E-mail to author from Kari Sandvik, cultural representative for *Krødsherad Kommune*, March 15, 2005.

3   The *e* at the end of the name was added in the United States, although there are two tombstones in the Snarum cemetery on which the name is spelled Svendsbye.

4   Author's June 9, 2001, conversation with Ove Brunes, husband of author's cousin Marit Svendsby, who now occupies the Svendsby farm home.

5   First- and second-class immigrants were examined and admitted to the United States before disembarking from the Celtic.

6   The poem is displayed only inside the pedestal, except in editorial cartoons and other results of artistic license.

7   In 1985, scientists at Bell Laboratories in New Jersey used emission spectography to analyze separate samples of copper from the statue and from the Visnes mine on the island of Karmöy, on Norway's west coast. They concluded that it was highly probable that both samples came from the Norwegian mine. See "Folklore Helps to Solve Miss Liberty's Mystery," *New York Times*, Dec. 30, 1985, B-1 (late city final edition).

8   Letter from May Birkelo to Inga Birkelo, November 18, 1935.

9   "Mrs. Thor Birkelo," Wildrose Mixer, January 10, 1939; "Thor S. Birkelo," *Wildrose Mixer*, January 16, 1941.

10   Original Monthly Record of Observations at New York, New York, for July 1904, in archives of the National Climatic Data Center, Asheville, North Carolina.

11   Ellis Island, Ship Manifest, Passenger Record. To view Ellis Island records for Anders Svendsbye, go to the Ellis Island Foundation's Web site: www.ellisisland. org. Using the site's basic (not advanced) passenger search, type in only Svendsby (no e) in the last-name box, then click on search. From the results, select Anders Anderson Svendsby. Registration, which is free, is required to view passenger records, ship manifests, and ship images.

12   The Pennsylvania Railroad's tunnels from New Jersey to Manhattan and from Manhattan to Long Island would not be completed for several years. Until then, passengers leaving Manhattan on the Pennsylvania Railroad headed west would have taken a ferry across the Hudson to Jersey City.

13   Although homesteading and naturalization were matters of U.S. rather than state law, the legal steps for both most often took place in state and even county courts. Williams County was in North Dakota's Sixth Judicial District 1889–1903, the Eighth 1903–1911, and the Eleventh beginning in 1911. Ward County (with Minot its county seat) was in the Second 1889–1903, then in the Eighth. Today both counties are in the state's Northwest Judicial District. As Robinson points out, North Dakota's county courts mostly handle probate matters but also have concurrent jurisdiction with the district courts in some lesser civil and criminal matters. See Robinson, *History of North Dakota,* 214.

14   Naturalization Record of Anders A. Svendsbye, North Dakota Eighth Judicial District, November 17, 1904.

15   Non-Mineral Affidavit, North Dakota Eighth District Court, November 17, 1904.

16   Homestead Affidavit, North Dakota Eighth District Court, November 17, 1904.

17   Marlene Eide, *Wonder of Williams: A History of Williams County, North Dakota,* p. 1616.

Chapter 2

1   See Eide, *Wonder of Williams,* 1:1881–1936; Marlene Knutson, *History of Tioga: Tioga Jubilee,* 1902–1977 (Tioga, North Dakota: [jubilee committee], 1977).

2   Minutes, Williams County Commissioners, November 15, 1909.

3   Minutes, Williams County Commissioners, January 6, 1910, and February 14, 1910.

4   Thor Birkelo's Application to Amend before U.S. Land Office, Williston, North Dakota, December 5, 1905.

5   Anne Birkelo's Application to Amend before U.S. Land Office, Devils Lake, North Dakota, December 5, 1905. It is not clear why the name of Devils Lake is on the application form. The handwriting on Anne's application appears to be identical to the handwriting on Thor's application. Moreover, Anne and Thor have the same witnesses. Their documents are signed by the same person and dated the same day.

6   Memo from George Wilson, register, U.S. Land Office, Department of the Interior, Williston, North Dakota, September 7, 1906, to Anne Birkelo, addressed to her as "sir."

7   A comparison of court and Land Office documents provides an insight into office practices and use of technology a century ago. In North Dakota, the basic documents were printed and thus identical. The filled-in-spaces were hand or

type written by staff members of the various offices. The handwriting varied greatly. Sometimes it was clear and elegant. At other times it was barely legible, with spelling errors. Even the typing wasn't perfect. Typing errors were sometimes crossed out with an X. There appear to have been standard texts used for letters dealing with the same subject. In one letter, Anne Birkelo is referred to as "he."

8   Homestead Entry, Final Proof, Department of the Interior, U.S. Land Office, Williston, North Dakota, undated, but likely May 16, 1910.

9   Last will of Anne S. Birkelo, filed November 12, 1908, with Judge A. L. Butler, Williams County (North Dakota) Court.

10   Letter from Samuel Adams, register, Department of the Interior, U.S. Land Office, Williston, North Dakota, to commissioner, General Land Office, October 3, 1910.

11   United States of America Certificate of Naturalization, No. 126935, A. H. Brown, clerk, District Court, Williston, North Dakota, April 5, 1910.

12   Letter from Anders Svendsbye, Temple, North Dakota, to Elling Svendsbye, Snarum, Norway, June 25, 1914.

Chapter 3

1   See "Tioga North Dakota—'Oil Capital of North Dakota,'" www.tiogand.net.

2   *Williston Herald*, October 12, 1905.

3   Eide, *Wonder of Williams*, 1:811.

4   Ralph W. and Muriel Hidy, Roy V. Scott and on L. Hofsommer, *The Great Northern Railway: A History* (Minneapolis University of Minnesota Press, 1988) 59.

Chapter 4

1   See Daily Program and Classification Reports of the Hankey teachers to Williams County Superintendent of Schools, in archives of North Dakota Historical Society, Bismarck, North Dakota.

2   The storm was so extraordinary that more than a half century later, John M Andrist, former publisher of the *Tioga Tribune* wrote a special article for the Tribune about the storm on its sixty-fifth anniversary, in which he recounted his experience as a boy in Columbus, Burke County, North Dakota, to the northeast of Hamlet. Jon M. Andrist, "A Blizzard That Lives in Infamy," *Tioga Tribune*, p. 6, March 12, 2008.

3   Letter from Anders A. Svendsbye to Elling Andersen Svendsbye, Snarum, Norway, June 25, 1914.

4   Letter from Elling Andersen Svendsbye to Ole Svendsby, Snarum, Norway, March 17, 1929.

Chapter 5

1   These records are not available for examination because of the National Privacy Act.

2   Final Account in the matter of the Estate of Anne S. Birkelo before Judge A. L. Butler, Williams County Court, September 14, 1915.

3   Statement by K. S. Birkelo before M. S. Williams, receiver, U.S. Land Office, Williston, North Dakota, March 16, 1910.

4   Letter to John Meblank, acting commissioner, Department of the Interior, General Land Office, Washington, D.C., from K. S. Bjerkelo, Edinburg, North Dakota, February 18, 1911.

5   Certificate by G. W. Wilson, register, Department of Interior, U.S. Land Office, May 24, 1910.

6   M. P. LeRoy, secretary, and H. W. Sanford, recorder, General Land Office, Washington, D.C., May 18, 1911.

7   Final Account in Matter of the Estate of Anne S. Birkelo before Judge A. L. Butler, Williams County Court, September 8, 1915.

8   Robinson, *History of North Dakota*, 400.

9   Robinson, *History of North Dakota,* 400.

10 Letter from L. Dennen, attorney at law, April 20, 1932, to A. A. Svendsbye.

11 Letter from V. E. Bahr, Equitable Collection Agency, October 30, 1930, to Anders A. Svendsbye.

12 Letter from Simon-Berg Co., Inc, (no signature), to A. Swnsby [sic], Aug. 30, 1921.

13 Robinson, *History of North Dakota*, 408.

14 Letter from E. A. Wilson, Federal Emergency Relief Administration for North Dakota and executive director, North Dakota Public Welfare Board, September 7, 1935, to Andrew [sic] Svendsby.

15 Letter from M. D. Avery, president, Federal Land Bank of St. Paul, July 21, 1952, to Anders A. Svendsbye.

Chapter 6

1   Robinson, *History of North Dakota*, 405.

2   Robinson, *History of North Dakota*, 329. Early efforts to organize the Nonpartisan League were dramatized in the 1978 film *Northern Lights*, written and directed by John Hanson and Rob Nilsson and filmed at Crosby, North Dakota, some thirty miles north of Wildrose. The film opens with the recollections of the real-life Henry Martinson, then ninety-four, who homesteaded in the state, was secretary of the Socialist Party, and for twenty-eight years was the state's labor commissioner. The movie won a Golden Camera award for best first film at the 1979 Cannes Film Festival in France.

3   Robinson, *History of North Dakota*, 397.

4   Minutes, Williams County Commissioners, February 15, 1910.

5   I matriculated at Concordia College, Moorhead, Minnesota, in 1947 and gradu-
     ated in the spring of 1951. To pay my college expenses, I had two scholarships,
     a $150 first-semester tuition scholarship from the college as a freshman and
     a $1,000 leadership scholarship from Lutheran Brotherhood as a senior. My
     parents loaned me $1,800, which I later repaid. The rest I earned working for
     the college for 30 cents an hour working in the college cafeteria, $1.00 an hour
     working as a night watchman for an elevator, and at the *Fargo Forum*, where
     I worked for Northwest Editor Lloyd Sveen as a writer for 90 cents an hour.
     Those sources, plus a variety of summer work, provided enough money to pay
     all my college expenses.

6   Robinson, History of North Dakota, 3.

7   Colleen A. Oihus, A History of Coal Mining in North Dakota, 1873-1982 (Grand
     Forks, North Dakota Geological Survey, Educational Series 15, 1983) 1.

Chapter 7

This chapter is more a memoir than a history. My memory, however, has been checked
against the memory and date of other family members so that I believe the memoir
is highly accurate.

Chapter 8

This chapter is a memoir also, but is written without consultation with any family
members. The evaluations and judgments made of my parents, teachers, the church,
the quality of education offered, and any other matters are mine alone.

Acknowledgments

A number of people have been helpful to me in this project, for which I am deeply grateful. Two people in particular helped me conceptualize what I wanted to do. They are Dr. Todd Nichol, King Olav V Professor of Scandinavian–American Studies at St. Olaf College, Northfield, Minnesota, and Dr. Peter T. Harstad, past director of the State Historical Society of Iowa and past executive director of the Indiana Historical Society. Dr. Don L. Hofsommer, professor of history at St. Cloud State University, St. Cloud, Minnesota, was very encouraging about this project and was particularly helpful in our discussion about the railroads. Dr. Ross F. Collins, from the North Dakota Institute for Regional Studies, was also very helpful in the comments he shared.

My siblings, who read portions of the manuscript, made careful and helpful observations. They are Adeline Elverud, Edward Svendsbye, and Jean Brusven. In addition, two nephews, Kenneth and Marlyn Vatne, were helpful in providing information and discussing certain historical questions about the Hamlet area. I was assisted in a beautiful way on some research by Adrienne Stepanek, director of Dakota Research at Williston, North Dakota.

Donn McLellan, free-lance editor, did the first review of the document, and Todd Nichol did the second. Both left their insightful marks on the manuscript. I am especially indebted to two additional people. Leonard Flachman, publisher of Lutheran University Press, was particularly wise in his editorial and publisher decisions. And my wife, Annelotte, was my close advisor and editor from the inception of this project until its completion in her characteristically gentle and incisive manner.

Index